Little
sew
& sew

Little Sew & Sew

OVER 30 DELIGHTFULLY SIMPLE SEWING AND EMBROIDERY PROJECTS

Christine Leech

Quadrille
PUBLISHING

Photography by Keiko Oikawa

WHAT'S INSIDE?

Contents

How to use this book

There are over 50 embroidery patterns within this book, so even when you've made all the sewing projects and are looking for more inspiration, there are plenty of ways to keep stitching. Embellish existing cushion covers with the Woodland Storage Boxes patterns (see page 34), embroider your fabric shopping bag with a cheery elephant (see page 54) or embroider a set of initialled placemats for each member of your family and friends (see page 108).

Many of the embroidery patterns comprise several separate elements, so if you only want to use the flowers from the Bunny Wash Day Peg Bag (see page 44) or one sheep from the Counting Sheep Pillow (see page 102), that's up to you. You could embroider for five minutes or five days and still have a pretty little something to show at the end.

There's something for everyone in this book. If you are a novice, the Kissing Kids Shoulder Bag (see page 68) uses just two types of stitch and rectangles of fabric so it's really simple to complete. If you are looking for something to get your teeth into, the Alphabet Wall Hanging (see page 108) will keep you going for a while!

Several of the projects in this book work brilliantly as freestyle embroidery patterns. Once you've got the outline of your elephant cushion (see page 54) planned, then how you embroider her is up to you. You could just decorate her with simple lazy daisy stitches or go all out and cover all the fabric in delicate lines of stitches. The Ribbon Allium Bag (see page 76) looks stunning with its big pompom flower heads, but lots of smaller flower heads would be equally effective.

Introduction

When I was very young, I entered my village's Flower and Produce Show and won first prize for 'Neatest Hemmed Handkerchief' (I have the certificate to prove it!). I remember sitting with my Nanny in the dark front room of our seaside holiday house in Margate, stitching and unpicking the hem to get the stitches as neat and straight as I could.

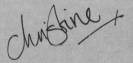

That is where my love of embroidery and sewing began. At school I made trousers from the itchiest grey fabric I've ever worn (from the bargain bin in the local fabric shop). In my early teens I embroidered my own cloth badges, which I proudly sewed on to my jeans and rucksack, proclaiming my love of bands such as Bros and T'Pau. In my final school years, I started making a patchwork quilt; I finally finished it 15 years later when I moved into my first home and needed a new bed covering. At university I made fancy dress outfits and leopard-print fake fur hats for all my housemates, and every year someone gets a home-made hot water bottle cover (I wonder who will receive the embroidered one from page 48 this year?).

So I guess you could say I have been sewing all my life, picking up tips and tricks from my mother, grandmothers and aunts – all great sewers. This book, with 16 sewing projects and over 50 embroidery patterns, has enabled me to combine my love of doodling (and made my illustration degree worthwhile), my love of solving problems and my love of making pretty things.

In the middle of making this book I moved house, so several of the projects came from a real need to nest. The Bunny Wash Day Peg Bag (see page 44) and the Woodland Storage Boxes (see page 34) were put to work as soon as I finished them! And Nelly the embroidered elephant cushion (see page 54) has pride of place on my new sofa. When I was deep in the midst of 'General House Move Horrors' and solicitors were haggling over moving dates, I was happily ensconced in a world of embroidery silks and stitches. The rhythmic, repetitive movement of the needle relaxed me and transported me into a calm, meditative state of mind, so if you're looking for some 'me' time, embroidery is the new yoga!

I hope you will enjoy making the projects in this book as much as I did.

Christine x

Embroidery kit essentials

My embroidery kit is made up of a mixture of finds from car boot sales, hand-me-downs from my Nanny and Great Aunt and new-fangled accessories designed to make an embroiderer's life easier.

EMBROIDERY FLOSSES

Embroidery flosses come in pretty much every colour you could ever want, plus metallics, neon, graduated tones, and even glow-in-the-dark options! They are sold by the skein (each skein is roughly 8m long). All flosses are identified by number rather than a colour name – there is such a gradual variation in colour that it would be impossible to give a name to every colour (and they wouldn't fit on the packaging)! Each manufacturer has its own set of unique numbers to identify the colours. In this book, if you want to embroider a project in the exact colourway I have used, follow the DMC brand numbers listed. However, I have also given a generic colour name if you have other brands of floss.

You can buy colour charts that have every colour a manufacturer makes – these are great reference tools to have at home when planning projects (I often find I am overwhelmed when I see the giant spinners of floss in the shops and completely forget which colours I need, coming home with shades almost identical to the ones I already have!). There are also online colour conversion charts (see page 126 for web links), which will help you to find the equivalent floss colour from different manufacturers.

A skein of floss is made up of six thin strands (called plies) twisted together to make a thicker floss. You can split the skein into separate plies to give different thicknesses to your embroidered design. Most of the projects in this book use four plies of thread, but please check the instructions for each project before you begin.

It's good to get into the habit of storing your threads as neatly as possible. I keep mine in small transparent sandwich bags, grouping similar colours together. When I have inevitably broken the thin paper bands holding the skein together, I wind the floss onto small pieces of card I have cut out using a paper punch in the shape of a flower (remember to write the colour number on the card). Not only is this a pretty shape, but the notches keep the thread tidy and in place. I'd like to say I do this with all my flosses, but that's not the case! It is a theraputic exercise though. Some embroiderers like to use wooden clothes pegs, or you can buy ready-cut embroidery cards and a special winding machine to make it easier.

OTHER EMBROIDERY THREADS

You don't have to limit yourself to using only embroidery floss. Tapestry wools or standard knitting wool work well on felt and fairly open-weave wool fabrics. As these wools are thicker than regular floss, you will need a bigger needle and a more freestyle, less detailed pattern.

RIBBONS

Embroidering with ribbons is a great alternative when creating flowers and simple shapes. Ribbons measuring between 2mm and 15mm in width work best. Do experiment with all kinds as they can all give different effects, although I find softer ones, such as gauze and silk, are easiest to work with. Make sure you don't try to embroider on to a very stiff fabric as it can be tricky to pull the ribbon through if the weave is too tight.

EMBROIDERY HOOPS

At the last count I had eight hoops, ranging from tiny (10cm diameter) to large (30cm diameter). For the majority of the projects in this book I used a medium-sized hoop of 20cm. I find the fabric gets baggy in the centre when using larger hoops, and you have to keep moving the smaller ones around if your design is larger than the hoop (although small ones are more portable, and good for train journeys as they take up less space in your bag).

Wooden hoops are great for displaying finished work as they are aesthetically pleasing, but your fabric can tend to slip slightly when sewing, so make sure you have tightened the screw firmly. With all hoops, keep the fabric taut at all times. Plastic and metal hoops can hold the fabric in place more securely as they have a lip. When placing the fabric in the hoop you should have approximately 7cm of excess fabric hanging on all sides.

If you are using a wooden hoop, first separate the hoop so you have two pieces. Place the inner hoop on a flat surface and lay your fabric over the top (with the embroidery pattern centered). Place the outer hoop over the fabric and inner hoop, tighten the screw and tease the fabric out at the sides until the fabric is taut.

If you have a metal and plastic hoop, separate the plastic circle from the metal round by pinching the two metal levers together. Keeping these levers pinched, place the fabric over the metal and place the plastic circle on top, then slowly release the levers to sandwich the fabric between the metal and plastic hoops. Pull the fabric taut.

NEEDLES

A variety pack of embroidery needles (also known as crewel needles) of different sizes will have all the needles you need. Good embroidery needles are sharp with a long eye (which allows space for several plies). Don't use a massive needle with thin embroidery thread on fine material as you'll end up with visible holes in the fabric.

PINS

I never seem to have as many pins when I finish a project as when I start, which can't be a good thing! So I'm beginning to find a pin cushion invaluable. A strip of magnetic tape stuck to your sewing machine is a great place to store pins when machine stitching.

Long, flat-headed pins are the best to use if they are going under your sewing machine plate and needle and always place them at right angles to your stitch line so that the machine needle will pass over them. Stainless steel pins are recommended as they do not rust or mark the fabric.

SCISSORS AND CUTTING IMPLEMENTS

A small, sharp pair of embroidery scissors with pointed blades is useful for snipping away leftover floss. A good pair of fabric scissors is a great investment, but don't be tempted to use them for cutting anything other than fabric, or they will soon lose their sharpness. Mine inevitably start off as fabric scissors, then sooner or later cut the odd bit of paper and card, and finally end up in the kitchen drawer for cutting old rags, plant stems and bacon rind! I also use a Stanley knife or craft knife, metal ruler and cutting mat when I need to cut long straight edges of fabric. If you don't feel confident with a knife and ruler, then a rotary fabric cutter is also good (always use a cutting mat to protect your work surface and regularly change the blades so they don't get dull and start dragging on the fabric). Pinking shears or scallop-edged scissors add a pretty decorative edge to fabrics, but are best used on fabric that doesn't fray.

DESIGN TRANSFERRING TOOLS

There are several ways to transfer your chosen design onto fabric, and the method you use depends on the type and colour of the fabric. Tailor's chalk, a quilter's pencil or water-soluble or air-erasable pens are the easiest and least messy ways. If you choose an air-erasable pen, make sure you embroider quickly or use it on a smaller pattern as the design may fade before you finish (I know, it's happened to me!). See Transferring The Pattern on page 12 for more information.

OTHER USEFUL BITS AND BOBS

A needle threader can be useful if you find it tricky to feed the floss through the eye of the needle and a thimble is good for protecting your index finger when sewing thicker fabric. Some people find embroiderer's beeswax useful for lubricating floss to prevent it becoming tangled; it can also help metallic flosses go through the fabric more smoothly. You simply drag your floss across the beeswax cube, pressing it into the surface, which gives your floss a little coating of wax.

Ready to begin?

Now you have filled your sewing box, we need to get you started on a project. For this you will need some fabric and an embroidery design or pattern to follow.

TYPES OF FABRIC

You can embroider on almost much any fabric. Heavyweight fabrics, such as denim or cotton twill, are good to work with as they are stiff and may not need a hoop, but it can be hard work getting the needle through the fabric (this is where using a thimble can be handy). Be wary of using upholstery fabric as it may have been treated on the reverse with a type of plastic coating, which makes it tricky to get the needle through (in the past I've worked with a fabric where I had to use pliers to pull the needle out!).

Delicate fabric, like chiffon or silk, requires a thinner embroidery thread (maybe just two or three plies) and a small needle. Be careful that your design doesn't weigh the fabric down or distort it, and if the fabric is a pale colour or see-through, try to be neat with the reverse of your embroidery as it may show through.

Embroidering on stretchy fabric (such as T-shirt material or fleece) is tricky as it can be pulled out of shape when placed in a hoop. Use a fabric stabiliser to support the fabric. Stabilisers come in a variety of forms, including iron on, spray on, tear away and water soluble. If you use a stretch fabric, follow the manufacturer's recommendations for the type of stabiliser you choose.

Most of the projects in this book use mediumweight linen or cotton. Linen comes in a variety of thicknesses and colours, and it benefits from having a loose weave so the needle travels through it nicely. The grid-like structure of the weave helps you maintain an even stitch length.

TRANSFERRING THE PATTERN

There are several different ways to transfer the embroidery design on to your chosen fabric. These are the methods used in this book.

Water-soluble or air-erasable pen

This method is the easiest way to transfer a design on to the fabric (unless you are drawing freehand). It works best with light- to mediumweight fabrics in pale or mid-tone colours as you can easily see through the fabric when you hold it up to a light source. First, trace or photocopy your chosen design on to paper. Place the paper and the fabric on a light box or tape to a sunny window (with the fabric uppermost) and trace the design on to the fabric. Use a couple of pieces of sticky tape to hold the fabric and design in place. This is especially helpful if your design is large and you are using a window as your light source as this can be quite tiring on your arms. Remember that the air-erasable 'ink' will fade in time (see page 10). Water-soluble 'ink' can be dabbed away with a barely damp cloth.

Tacking the design

The hot water bottle cover on page 48 uses a more traditional way of transferring the pattern. The fabric I chose for this is a slightly fluffy wool in a dark colour, so neither of the above methods were suitable.

Copy the design on to a thin paper (such as tissue paper), then tack the tissue paper to the fabric. Place the fabric and the paper into your embroidery hoop and roughly stitch the design through both layers using sewing thread (not embroidery thread) in a contrasting colour. Use a long top stitch and short bottom stitch so the pattern is quite visible. When finished, gently tear away the tissue paper and you will see the design on the fabric. Embroider over these tacked lines and carefully remove the tacking thread when finished.

Tailor's carbon paper

Also known as dressmaker's carbon paper, this comes in packs, usually with a variety of different coloured sheets – the one I use has white, yellow, blue and red. Tailor's carbon paper is less inky and messy than old-fashioned stationer's carbon paper and can be reused several times. This method of transferring designs works best on dark or thick material. Place your material on a hard surface, lay the carbon paper chalky side down on the fabric and your chosen design on top. Tape the three layers to the work surface to prevent them moving. Using a ballpoint pen or similar blunt instrument, copy the design. The lines can rub and fade away as you embroider, so when possible (i.e. on lighter-coloured fabrics) I tend to go over the lines with a water-soluble pen before I start.

TOP TIP

Wash and iron your fabric before you cut it out and begin embroidering. It's far better for the fabric to shrink now than after you've finished your masterpiece!

USING EMBROIDERY FLOSS

Most of the designs in this book use four plies of thread. There are two ways to secure your thread when starting sewing. The first method is simply to make a small knot in the end of the embroidery floss. However, the second method (shown on the right), which I prefer, gives you a neater reverse.

Throughout the book you will find instructions for sewing a variety of embroidery stitches. Straight stitch (shown on the far right) is the simplest stitch and can be used to create different patterns – see overleaf for zigzag stitch and straight stitch leaves.

Finishing a line of stitching

Make sure you have enough floss left when finishing to secure the floss so it doesn't unravel later (see right for instructions on how to finish sewing without using a knot – this will give a smoother finish to your embroidery).

When you have finished embroidering, sponge the fabric to remove any traces of a transfer pen (if you have used one) and press with a damp towel on the reverse to remove any creases. Ironing on the reverse is always best as it won't scorch or flatten the embroidery floss.

To start sewing without a knot

* Take a piece of thread twice the length that you need (a length of around 40cm is comfortable to work with, any longer and it's all too easy to tangle the floss, any shorter and you could be constantly starting new bits of floss). Split the thread so you end up with half the number of plies needed for the project. For example, if a project recommends using six plies of floss, split your floss in half so you have two sets of three plies.
* Place one set of plies aside for later use. Fold the other set in half and thread all the raw ends through the needle. You now have floss of six plies again, with a loop at end.
* Push your needle into the fabric and draw the thread through until only the small loop is left on the reverse.
* Come back through the fabric using a very small stitch and thread your needle through the middle of the loop.
* Pull until tight and the loop is flat in the fabric. This will secure your thread with no messy knots.

To finish sewing without a knot

* As with starting your embroidery, you can also finish without a knot, making the reverse of your embroidery tider than if you simply knotted your floss.
* On the reverse of your embroidery, thread your needle and floss through the last stitch you completed but don't pull tight.
* Next pass the needle and floss throught the loop left and gently pull tight. This will secure the floss.

Straight stitch

* The simplest embroidery stitch is the straight stitch. It can be done at any length in any direction. Used close together it can quickly fill areas and make solid blocks of colour.
* To make a cross stitch, sew one straight stitch at a diagonal then another crossing it.
* There are lots of different stitches that are made up from the simple straight stitch – see the following pages, or create your own variations.

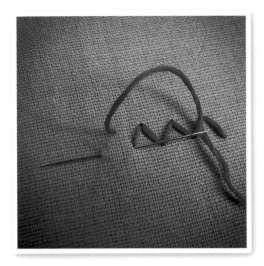

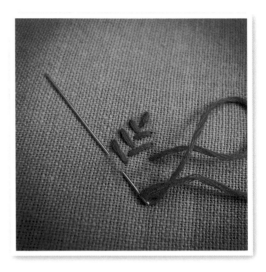

Zigzag stitch
* This is a nice decorative stitch, good for straight lines.
* Bring the needle up from the reverse of the fabric at A.
* Bring the needle back down at B, then out again at C.
* For the next stitch, push the needle back down at A, bring it out at D, then back in at C. Continue.

Straight stitch leaves
* Use small straight stitches at angles to create leaf shapes. First, draw a leaf shape and centre stem on your fabric with a water-soluble pen.
* Sew a small vertical stitch along the centre line at the tip of your leaf. Bring the needle out at one edge of the drawn outline (A), then back into the fabric on the centre line slightly lower down to make the stitch angled (B).
* Bring the needle back out on the opposite side of the leaf outline (C) and repeat, following the shape of the leaf.

OVER STITCH
* This stitch is useful for fixing little pieces of appliqué or decorations like ribbons and lace in place.
* Bring your needle and floss up from the reverse of your fabric just beyond the edge of the decoration you want to attach. Bring the needle down again through the decoration and the fabric. Repeat.
* It is often easier to fix the appliqué shape or decoration in place with a little fabric glue or Bondaweb first.

* Varying the lengths
of your running stitch
can give many
different effects.

* For two-colour running stitch, sew one line of
running stitch, then another in a different colour.

How to embroider ...
Running
& back stitch

B   A   C

BACK STITCH
* On the reverse of your fabric
sew a small straight stitch, bringing
the needle out at A.
* Put your needle back in at B,
then bring it out at C.
* Put it back in at A and repeat,
continuing in a line.

For the home

* Bird cage tea cosy
* Stripy seat cushion
* Woodland storage boxes
* Bunny wash day peg bag
* Scandi hot water bottle
* Nelly cushion

Bird cage tea cosy

This bird cage has no door, so the brightly coloured birds are free to come and go as they like, as all birds should. Right now, they are staying put for teatime.

For the embroidery

18cm diameter embroidery hoop

DMC stranded embroidery thread in the following colours:

white (shown as grey on the stitch diagram)

Top bird: peppermint 959, lime 3819, blue 312, grey 3072

Bottom bird: peach 353, pink 3689, lime 3819, dark pink 892

For the tea cosy

Two 50 x 50cm squares of mediumweight linen fabric

Two 50 x 50cm squares of patterned linen or cotton, for lining

1m x 50cm batting, 5mm thick, for insulation

Sewing thread to match the linen

TO EMBROIDER THE COSY

1. Use the cosy template on pages 122–123 at a size to suit your teapot. For an average six-cup teapot, use at the size shown.

2. Place the template on the linen, making sure there is at least 10cm all around to enable the fabric to stay in your embroidery hoop. Draw around the template, then tack with a brightly coloured thread around the line (use a tacking stitch about 1cm long so you can clearly see the shape of the cosy on both sides).

3. Transfer the birds from page 23 on to the fabric. If your fabric is light in colour, trace through using a water-soluble pen. If you are using a darker fabric, use tailor's carbon paper. (See pages 12–13 for methods.)

CONT. >>>

4. Use four plies of floss to embroider the birds following the stitch guide opposite. It is easy to draw the cage freehand – for reference, see the photograph on the previous page. Use six plies of floss for the cage and a long backstitch (see page 17). Sponge out the pen lines, if necessary, and press.

TO MAKE THE COSY

5. To make the hanging loop, cut two 3 x 18cm rectangles from the linen and lining fabric. Pin together with right sides facing. Sew around three sides, leaving one short end open, turn right side out and fold in half to create the loop. Press.

6. Place the embroidered front on a flat work surface, right side up. Place the loop at the centre of the top of the cosy so that the majority of the loop is facing downwards on the cosy and 1cm overlaps the tacked line.

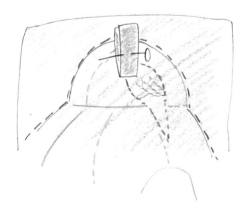

7. Place the back of the cosy on top of this, right side down, pin together and turn over. Machine stitch around the tacked line, over the loop and leave the bottom open. Cut away the excess fabric, leaving approximately 5mm all around.

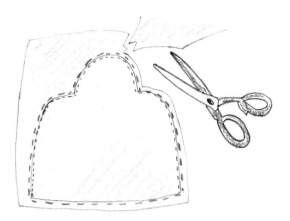

8. Cut small notches in the fabric where the cage curves – this will help the fabric stretch around the curves better. Remove any stray tacking threads, turn and press. (The loop will pop out when you turn the cosy right side out in step 11.)

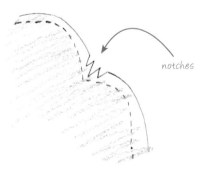

notches

CONT. 》》》

cross stitch

split stitch

STITCHES USED

Cross stitch (see page 15)
French knots (see page 93)
Split stitch (see page 25)

french knots

french knots

split stitch

9. Trace around the cosy shape onto one piece of the lining material, pin to the second piece and cut out, leaving a 2cm seam allowance all around. Place together, right sides facing, and mchine stitch together, leaving the bottom edge open. Trim close to the sewing line and notch around the curves.

10. Turn the outer cosy inside out. Keep lining right side out. Place the lining inside the outer cosy so that right sides are facing. Tack or pin the bottom edges together on each side and then sew. Leave a 12cm turning hole on each side.

11. Turn inside out through the turning holes and manipulate the fabrics so that the lining is inside the outer cosy – you shouldn't see any raw seams. Press the edge and turning holes.

12. Cut out two cosy shapes from the batting, making them 1cm smaller all around than the template. Insert the batting through the openings and flatten out between the lining and outer fabric. Hand stitch the openings closed. Press with a damp cloth.

embroidered case
inside out

lining
right side out

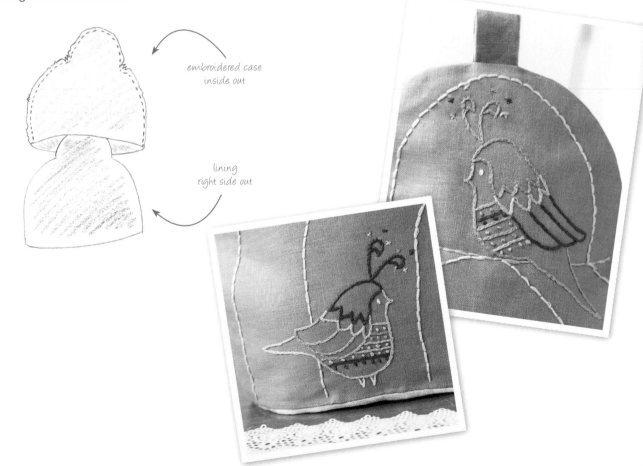

CHAIN STITCH

* Bring your needle through the fabric from the rear at A.
* Return the needle into the fabric slightly to the side at B.
* Loop the floss around your needle and insert back into the fabric at C. Repeat.

How to embroider...
Chain & split stitch

SPLIT STITCH

* Sew a small straight stitch.
* To make the next stitch, bring the needle up from beneath the fabric through the floss of the previous stitch, to split the stitch. Repeat.

Stripy seat cushion

This seat pad is a great way to practise your embroidery stitches. The grey and white ribbons and jumbo-sized ricrac add an extra decorative element, but lines of different embroidery stitches would look just as effective.

For the embroidery

50cm lengths of the following:

yellow ricrac ribbon, 2cm wide

grey satin ribbon, 1.5cm wide

white satin ribbon, 1cm wide

grey grosgrain ribbon, 2.5cm wide

grey spotty ribbon, 1.5cm wide

white grosgrain ribbon, 2.5 cm wide

grey and yellow striped ribbon, 1.5cm wide

DMC stranded embroidery thread in the following colours:

white, grey 317, yellow 973

For the seat pad

50cm square of grey linen or cotton

50cm square of yellow linen or cotton

1m ribbon, for ties

50cm square 15mm thick foam

Wonderweb

TO MAKE THE SEAT PAD

1. To make your own seat pad, first make a pattern. Place a piece of newspaper on the chair and draw around the shape of the chair seat on the paper – there may be a bit of trial and error until you get it right. For a symmetrical shape, fold the paper in half before cutting it out. Allow an extra 2cm all around the pattern to allow for the thickness of the foam and the seam allowance.

2. If you have a shop-bought seat pad, draw around the pad, measure the thickness of the pad and divide this measurement in half. Add this number all around the pattern (i.e. if the pad is 5cm thick, add 2.5cm all around the pattern plus an extra 1cm seam allowance).

3. Place your seat pattern on top of the grey fabric and draw around it using tailor's chalk or an air-erasable pen. Tack with a brightly coloured thread so you can see the shape of the cushion on both sides.

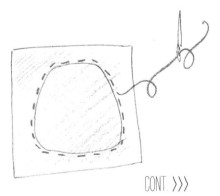

CONT. >>>

4. Lay out your ribbons and ricrac on the fabric following the embroidery pattern on page 30. Cut them about 2cm longer on each side than the cushion shape. Remember to leave enough space between the ribbons for your lines of embroidery.

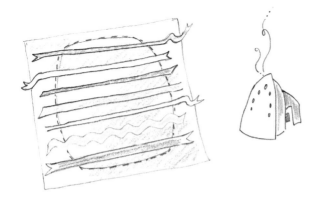

5. Cut strips of Wonderweb for each ribbon and follow the manufacturer's instructions to fix the ribbon and ricrac to the material. This makes it easier to embroider over them as they won't move around.

6. Using a ruler and an air-soluble pen or tailor's chalk, and referring to the embroidery guide overleaf, mark where the lines of embroidery will be. Using a full strand of floss, embroider the lines following the stitch guide overleaf. Make sure you continue the embroidery a couple of centimetres either side of the tacked cushion shape. Press.

7. Place the embroidered fabric on a flat work surface with right side up. Cut two 50cm lengths of ribbon for the cushion ties. Every chair is a little different so you will need to work out the best place for your ties to be placed so they will easily tie onto your chair. Fold each in half and pin in your desired place so the majority of the ribbon is downwards on the cushion and the folded section is overlapping the tacked line by 2cm. Place the back fabric on top of this and pin together.

8. Turn over and sew around the tacked line leaving the space between the two ribbons open. Trim away extra fabric, turn right side out and press, using a pressing cloth. Remove any visible tacking threads.

9. Cut a piece of foam 1cm smaller than the seat pattern and place inside the embroidered cover. Hand stitch the opening closed and tie to your chair with a couple of pretty bows.

CONT. >>>

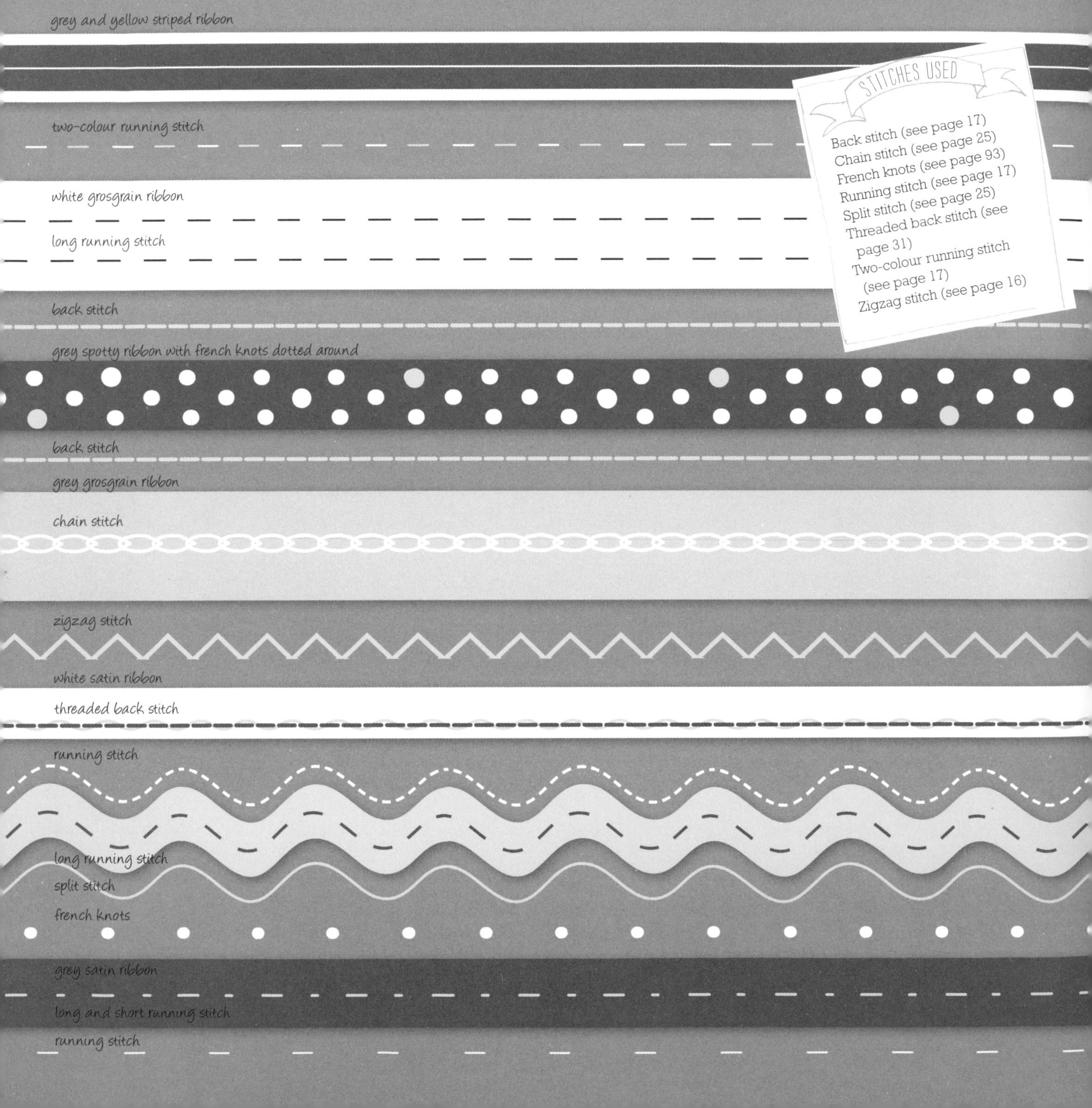
grey and yellow striped ribbon
two-colour running stitch
white grosgrain ribbon
long running stitch
back stitch
grey spotty ribbon with french knots dotted around
back stitch
grey grosgrain ribbon
chain stitch
zigzag stitch
white satin ribbon
threaded back stitch
running stitch
long running stitch
split stitch
french knots
grey satin ribbon
long and short running stitch
running stitch

STITCHES USED

Back stitch (see page 17)
Chain stitch (see page 25)
French knots (see page 93)
Running stitch (see page 17)
Split stitch (see page 25)
Threaded back stitch (see page 31)
Two-colour running stitch (see page 17)
Zigzag stitch (see page 16)

How to embroider ...
Threaded & looped stitches

THREADED RUNNING OR BACK STITCH
* You can make a variety of different stitches by threading a second thread through a line of running or back stitch. This second thread doesn't go though the fabric at any point – it just weaves though the stitches.

LOOPED BACK STITCH
* Loop a different coloured thread through a line of back stitch.

Woodland storage boxes

These boxes have an infinite number of uses. I like to keep ribbons and embroidery supplies in mine, but they would look great in a baby's room holding nappies, socks and bibs or in a bathroom storing all your toiletries.

For the embroidery

30cm diameter embroidery hoop

Anchor soft cotton thread in the following colours:

beige 386, cream 391 (use the whole skein as this thread is a twisted cotton and doesn't easily divide into plies)

For the boxes

150 x 50cm thick calico or cotton twill, for lining

150 x 50cm plain cotton twill for the outer fabric (make sure it's not too thick or you won't be able to embroider through it)

Cardboard, if you wish to stiffen your boxes

TO MAKE THE BOX LINING

1. Cut a 22 x 22cm square in calico or thick cotton (this includes a 1cm seam allowance) and a 84 x 22cm rectangle (also includes a 1cm seam allowance). Fold the rectangle in half lengthways to find the centre, then make a little mark here with tailor's chalk. Fold the square in half and make another mark. Line up the two marks and pin together, right sides facing inwards.

2. Pin the rest of the rectangle to the square base, then tack the base to the sides. The box sides will join in the middle of the far side edge. Tack up the short side.

3. Machine stitch the sides in place. It's easiest to do this if you keep the sides of the box uppermost. Leave a 10cm turning hole in one of the base sides (this will be easier if it's not the one with the join). Remove the tacking threads. Turn right side out so the raw edges are inside the box then press.

CONT. ⟩⟩⟩

USE TO STORE SEWING GOODIES, CRAFT ESSENTIALS OR EVEN KNICKERS & SOCKS!

NICE BOX

STITCHES USED

French knots (see page 93)
Running stitch (see page 17)
Satin stitch (see page 67)
Split stitch (see page 25)
Straight stitch (see page 15)
Straight stitch leaves (see page 16)

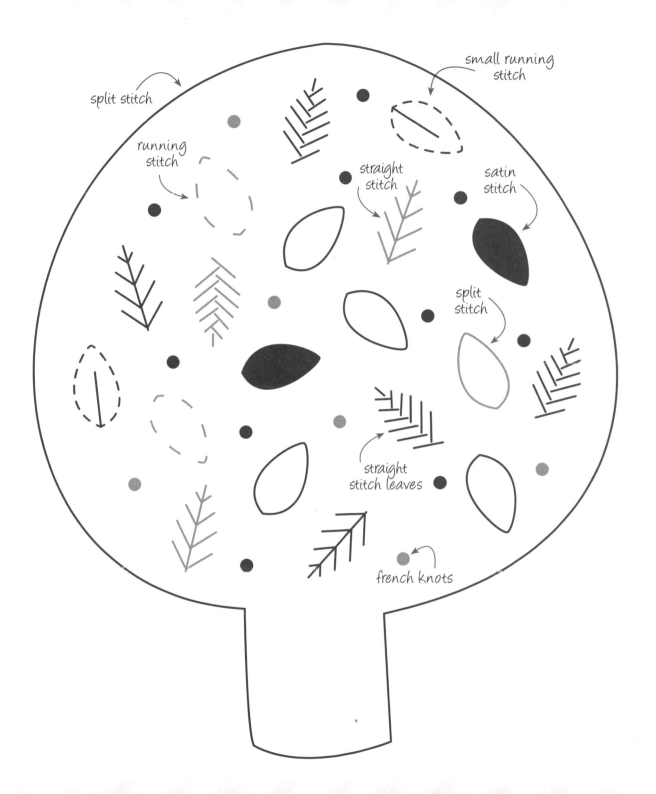

TO EMBROIDER THE DESIGN

4. For the embroidered outer box, mark out a 84 x 22 cm rectangle on the reverse of your fabric. Find the centre of the rectangle by folding in half lengthways, then measure 11cm either side of this and mark with tailor's chalk or a water-soluble pen – this forms the square panel that you will embroider. Cut around the rectangle with an allowance of 10cm fabric all around it so it fits securely in your embroidery hoop.

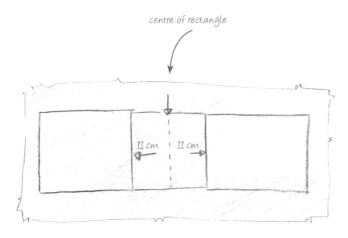

centre of rectangle

11 cm   11 cm

5. Choose the pattern you wish to embroider and trace on to thin paper. Transfer the pattern onto the fabric using tailor's carbon paper (see page 13). If the resulting pattern isn't quite clear enough to see, go over the lines with an air-erasable pen.

6. Place the fabric in the embroidery hoop and follow the stitch guide on pages 37, 38 or 41. When finished, press the fabric and use a damp cloth to remove any carbon or pen marks.

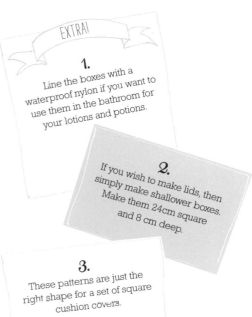

EXTRA!

1.
Line the boxes with a waterproof nylon if you want to use them in the bathroom for your lotions and potions.

2.
If you wish to make lids, then simply make shallower boxes. Make them 24cm square and 8 cm deep.

3.
These patterns are just the right shape for a set of square cushion covers.

STITCHES USED

Back stitch (see page 17)
Chain stitch (see page 25)
Lazy daisy (see page 87)
Running stitch (see page 17)
Split stitch (see page 25)

CONT. 〉〉〉

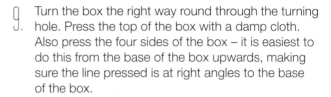

TO COMPLETE THE BOX

7. Trim the fabric to the drawn line. Cut out a 22 x 22cm square from the outer fabric and make up the box using the instructions for making the box lining (steps 1–3) but without leaving a turning hole.

8. Place the lining box inside the outer box that is still inside out (so the right sides of the boxes are facing each other). Line up the two rear seams, then pin the top of the boxes together. Sew around the box top. (If you want to reinforce the box sides, you can cut four 20cm squares of cardboard and insert them into the box through the turning hole – you will need to leave a larger hole and insert the card at step 10.)

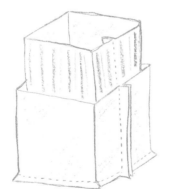

9. Turn the box the right way round through the turning hole. Press the top of the box with a damp cloth. Also press the four sides of the box – it is easiest to do this from the base of the box upwards, making sure the line pressed is at right angles to the base of the box.

10. Hand stitch the turning hole closed. To strengthen the box and enable it to keep its shape better, oversew each side of the box with blanket stitch (see page 59), sewing through the outer fabric and the lining of the box. Now find your boxes a home where they can be seen and admired, and get organising!

STITCHES USED

Back stitch (see page 17)
Chain stitch (see page 25)
Cross stitch (see page 15)
French knots (see page 93)
Lazy daisy (see page 87)
Running stitch (see page 17)
Scallop stitch (see page 59)
Split stitch (see page 25)
Stars (see page 53)
Straight stitch (see page 15)

Bunny wash day peg bag

When I started writing this book, I said I wouldn't make a peg bag as there are so many peg bag patterns out there. But then I moved house, acquired a garden and developed a desperate need for somewhere to keep my pegs!

SUPPLIES

For the embroidery

DMC stranded embroidery thread in the following colours:

red 321, dark brown 3860, yellow 727, petrol blue 3842, beige 3770, purple 327, pink 3708, lime green 907, light blue 3756, pale pink 353

16cm diameter embroidery hoop

Small scraps of coloured material for bunting appliqué

Scraps of Bondaweb

For the peg bag

Small wooden or plastic hanger

Paper and pencil

1m x 50cm linen or cotton

STITCHES USED

Back stitch (see page 17)
Cross stitch (see page 15)
French knots (see page 93)
Over stitch (see page 16)
Running stitch (see page 17)
Scallop stitch (see page 59)
Stars (see page 53)
Straight stitch (see page 15)
Tulips (see page 87)

TO MAKE THE BAG TEMPLATE

1. Draw around the body of your hanger (but not the hanging hook) on a piece of paper, then measure 13cm down from the highest point of the hanger and draw a horizontal line here. Extend the sides of the hanger down to this line. Fold the template in half vertically and cut out (this will give you a symmetrical template).

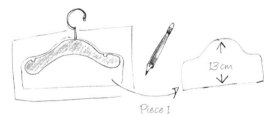

Piece 1

TO CUT OUT THE FABRIC

2. Place your template on the wrong side of your fabric and draw around it. Cut out, adding a 10cm allowance all around (to allow you to place the fabric securely in the embroidery hoop). This is piece 1.

3. To make the lower panel, place your hanger template on to the wrong side of your fabric and draw around it, then draw a 44cm long rectangle from the lower straight edge of the template. Cut out, adding a 10cm allowance all round. This is piece 2.

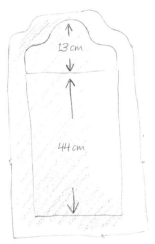

13 cm

44 cm

Piece 2

back stitch

applique bunting

over stitch

EMBROIDERY PATTERN A

4. Repeat steps 2 and 3 with your lining fabric, but cut them out with only a 1cm seam allowance all round.

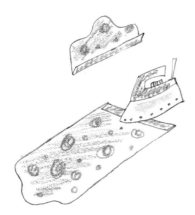

5. Turn up the short straight edge on the two lining fabric pieces by 1cm and press.

TO EMBROIDER THE DESIGN

6. Transfer embroidery pattern A (above) on to piece 1. Make sure the edges of the bunting line up with the edges of the drawn template. Transfer embroidery pattern B (see overleaf) to the lower half of piece 2, 10cm up from the bottom (make sure the washing line is touching the short edge of the rectangle).

7. To make the appliqué bunting, following the manufacturer's instructions, iron Bondaweb on to small scraps of fabric, then cut out bunting triangles approximately 2cm wide x 3cm deep or copy the bunting shown in the embroidery pattern. Iron these onto the fabric, then sew in place with a small over stitch (see page 16) using two plies of floss.

8. Following the stitch guide above and on pages 46–47, embroider the rest of the patterns. The majority of the embroidery uses a simple back stitch and four plies of floss. For the detailing on the clothes and the bunny and child's face, use two plies of floss for a more delicate stitch and follow the stitches shown. When you have finished, sponge off the transfer pen and press.

CONT. >>>

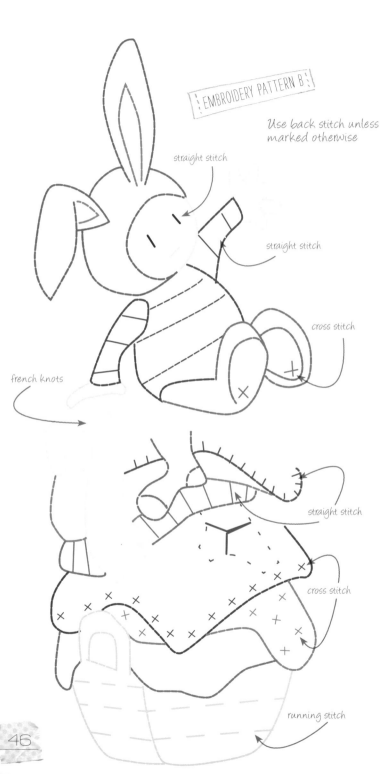

EMBROIDERY PATTERN B

Use back stitch unless marked otherwise

straight stitch

straight stitch

cross stitch

french knots

straight stitch

cross stitch

running stitch

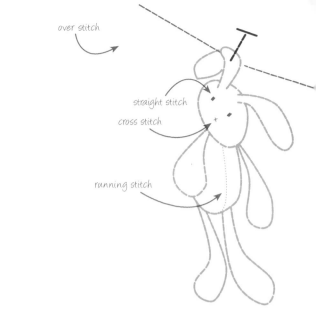

over stitch

straight stitch

cross stitch

running stitch

9. After embroidering, trim pieces 1 and 2 so they only have a 1cm seam allowance. Turn up by 1cm and press the short straight edge of each piece.

10. Lay piece 2 on a work surface with the embroidery facing up. Place piece 1 on piece 2 with its embroidery facing down and top curved edges aligning. Pin both pieces together, then fold the bottom of piece 2 up towards piece 1 so the two folded and pressed edges are touching. Pin the sides together, then machine stitch starting and stopping where shown below. Leave a 1cm hole in the top of the peg bag for the hanger hook. Repeat this step with the lining. Trim away any excess fabric.

hole for hanger hook

sew

sew

sew

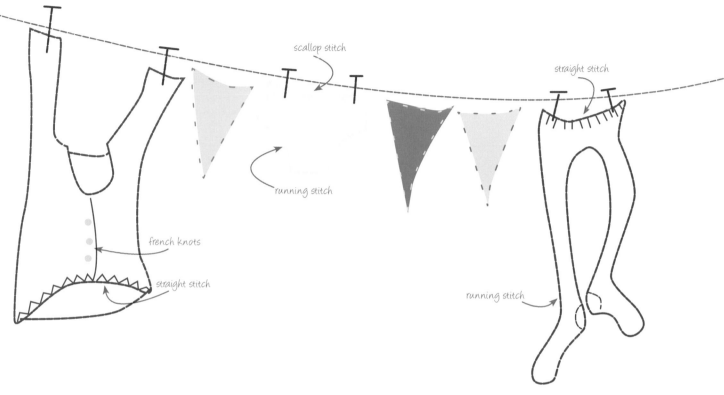

scallop stitch

straight stitch

running stitch

french knots

straight stitch

running stitch

11. You now have two bags. Turn the embroidered bag the right way round with the raw edges facing inwards. The lining bag should be inside out with the raw edges showing. Place the embroidered bag inside the lining bag (right sides together). Line up the four pressed edges of the opening, so the top two edges match, as do the bottom two.

12. Unfold the fabric of the pressed edges and pin the top two edges together (one lining and one outer) and the bottom two together, then machine stitch along the crease left by the ironed fold. Leave a 15cm turning gap in the lower edge.

13. Turn your bag inside out through the turning hole and rearrange the bag so the lining bag is inside the outer bag. Press, then hand stitch the turning gap closed.

14. Insert the hanger into the top of the peg bag and poke the hook through the hole. Fill with pegs and never have a boring wash day again!

star

appliqué circles

over stitch

french knots

tulips

Scandi hot water bottle

The symmetrical design of this hot water bottle cover is inspired by the striking needlework of Scandinavia. I have used a beautiful, dark cashmere wool, but white floss embroidered on red fabric would also work well.

For the embroidery

20cm diameter embroidery hoop

Tissue paper

DMC stranded embroidery thread in the following colours:

lilac 209, dark lilac 340, purple 791, violet light 554, blue violet 3746, light blue violet 341, wedgwood blue 3842, wedgwood light 518, light turquoise 958

For the hot water bottle cover

1m x 50cm piece of felt, wool cashmere or fleece

1m x 50cm piece of cotton for lining

Pinking shears

TO EMBROIDER THE DESIGN

1. Hot water bottles vary in size so check the size of yours and adjust the size of the template on pages 50–51 accordingly. Trace the pattern (including the outline) on to tissue paper.

2. Cut a piece of fabric 30 x 45cm. Pin the tissue paper onto the fabric and place both in your embroidery hoop. First tack the shape of the cover on to the fabric using a brightly coloured thread which will stand out against the background. Use long stitches on the reverse and short stitches on the front (this is the line you will follow when sewing the two sides of the case together).

3. Tack the pattern through the tissue paper onto the fabric. You don't need to tack all the pattern as the French knots, stars and lazy daisy stitches are easy to add later, so just tack the main pattern. Use long stitch on the upper side and short stitches on the reverse.

4. When finished, carefully tear away the tissue paper and you will see the rough pattern tacked on the fabric. Following the embroidery pattern and the stitch guide on pages 50–51, begin embroidering. Use a full strand of floss.

CONT. >>>

TO MAKE THE CASE

5. When finished embroidering, remove the fabric from the hoop and remove all the tacking threads. Press, using a damp pressing cloth.

6. Cut two rectangles from the same fabric, one measuring 23 x 30cm and the other 27 x 30cm. These will form the back of the hot water bottle cover. Pin and press a 5mm hem to the wrong side on one of the 30-cm sides of each rectangle.

7. Place the embroidered front piece on a work surface, embroidered side up. Place the smaller rectangle on top, right side down and with the top edges aligned, and then the larger one so the bottom edges line up. The two rectangles should overlap by approximately 4cm where they meet.

CONT. 〉〉〉

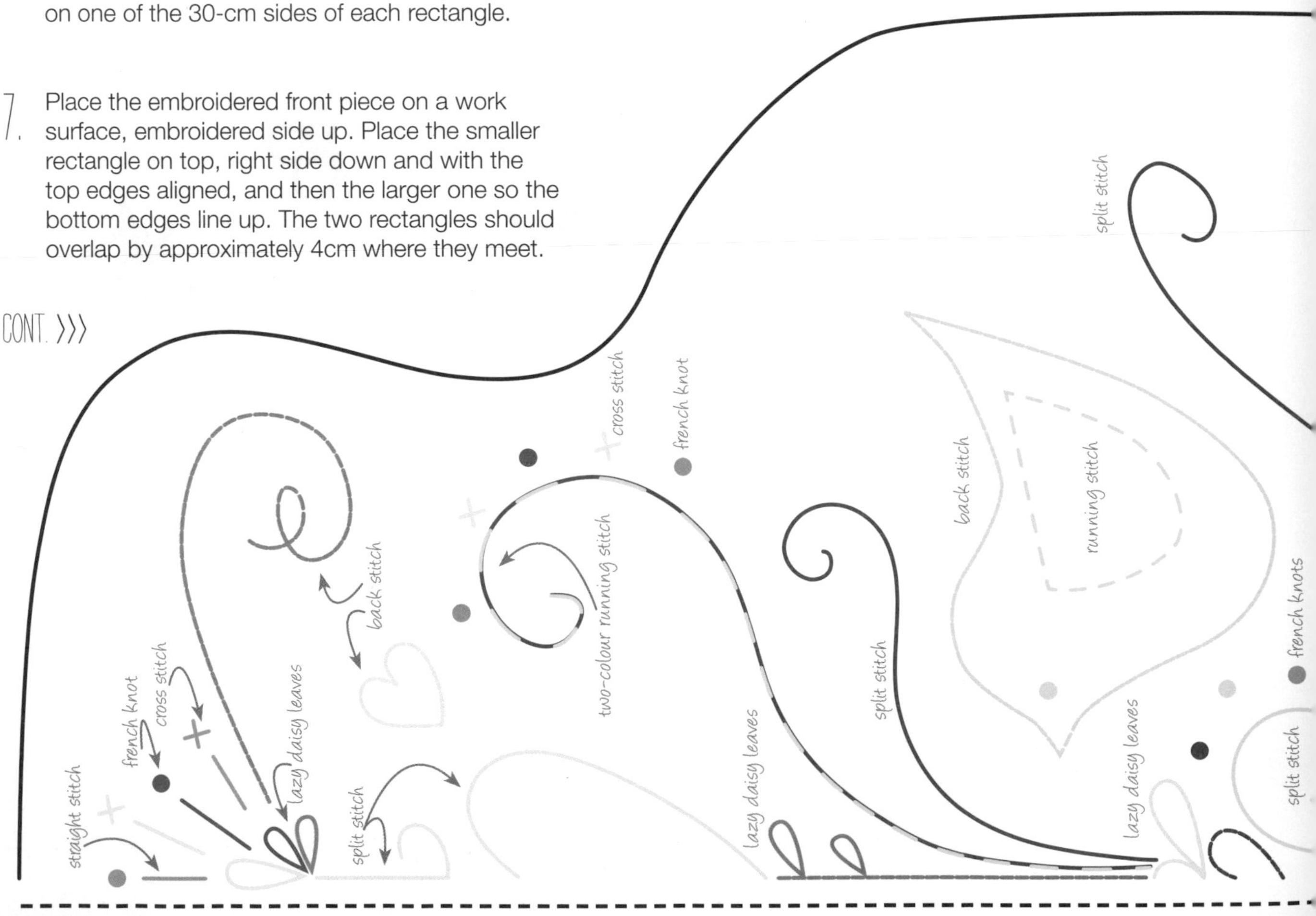

27 cm

23 cm

split stitch

cross stitch

french knot

back stitch

running stitch

two-colour running stitch

french knots

back stitch

cross stitch

french knot

split stitch

lazy daisy leaves

split stitch

lazy daisy leaves

lazy daisy leaves

split stitch

straight stitch

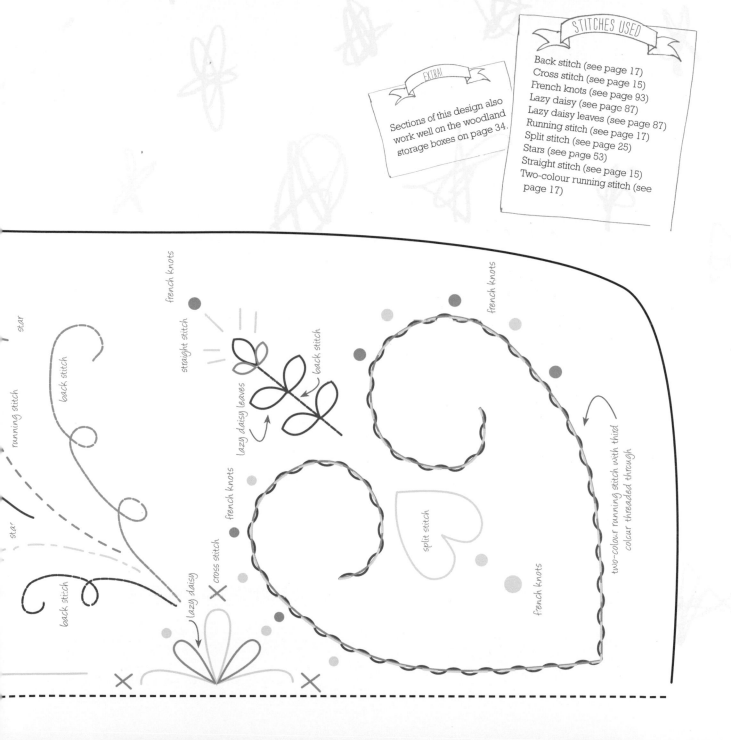

EXTRA!

Sections of this design also work well on the woodland storage boxes on page 34.

STITCHES USED

Back stitch (see page 17)
Cross stitch (see page 15)
French knots (see page 93)
Lazy daisy (see page 87)
Lazy daisy leaves (see page 87)
Running stitch (see page 17)
Split stitch (see page 25)
Stars (see page 53)
Straight stitch (see page 15)
Two-colour running stitch (see page 17)

french knots

french knots

star

back stitch

running stitch

straight stitch

back stitch

lazy daisy leaves

star

back stitch

back stitch

lazy daisy

cross stitch

french knots

french knots

split stitch

french knots

two-colour running stitch with third colour threaded through

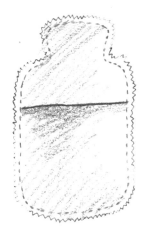

8. Pin all the rectangles together, then turn over and machine stitch all the way around the tacked case shape. Trim the case 1cm from the sewn line with pinking shears. Turn inside out, shape and press.

9. If you don't wish to line your case, finish off the opening edges with a blanket stitch (see page 59) to hold the turned open edges in place.

10. If you would like to line your case, make another case in the same way. Use a light coloured fabric and trace the case shape with an air-erasable pen or tailor's chalk. Machine stitch together, but this time sew 3mm inside the case outline and don't sew where the two rectangles overlap on the reverse of the case.

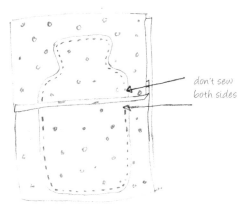

don't sew both sides

11. Trim the case close to the stitch line and then place inside the embroidered case. (Don't turn inside out as you want raw edges to be touching.)

12. Push the lining into place inside the embroidered cover, then line up the folded edges of the open sides of the lower cases. It's easiest to pin these together before you stitch. Use a blanket stitch to sew the lining and outer case together. Repeat with the upper cases.

13. Place your filled hot water bottle inside the case and have a cosy night's sleep.

STAR 1.
* Sew a straight stitch. The point where your needle enters the fabric will be the centre of the star.
* Repeat with 5 or 6 more stitches. Always stitch to the centre of the star.

How to embroider ...
Stars

STAR 2.
* Sew three straight stitches each overlapping in the middle.
* Experiment with different length stitches for variety.

Nelly cushion

This Nelly is a highly decorated elephant! You can either follow the stitch guide overleaf or create your own design and choose your own colours.

SUPPLIES

For the embroidery

20cm diameter embroidery hoop

DMC stranded embroidery thread in the following colours:

mint green 3849, peach 3341, pale green 3013, beige 822, sky blue 3810, orange 741, raspberry 891, yellow 3819, lilac 340, gold 832, metallic gold E3852

For the cushion

Two 50 x 50cm squares of linen

1m x 50cm cotton lining fabric

Cushion stuffing

TO EMBROIDER THE DESIGN

1. Enlarge the pattern on page 121 by 118% and cut out. Place the template on one of the squares of linen, pin in place and trace around using tailor's chalk or an air-erasable pen. Remove the template.

2. Using a brightly coloured thread, tack the outline of the elephant so you can see the shape on both sides of the fabric – this will be useful later, when sewing the cushion together.

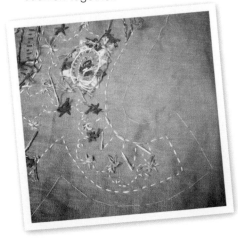

3. Copy the embroidery pattern overleaf on to the fabric using a water-soluble pen or tailor's chalk. When transferring the pattern, there is no need to copy every line on to your fabric. If you draw just her eye, ear, headpiece, saddle and the flowers, it is quite easy to free-style around these using different stitches following these basic guides. Place the linen in the embroidery hoop and embroider following the stitch guide on page 56. Use a full strand of floss.

4. When finished, sponge away the water-soluble pen or brush off the tailor's chalk and press flat, using a damp cloth to protect the embroidery floss.

CONT. >>>

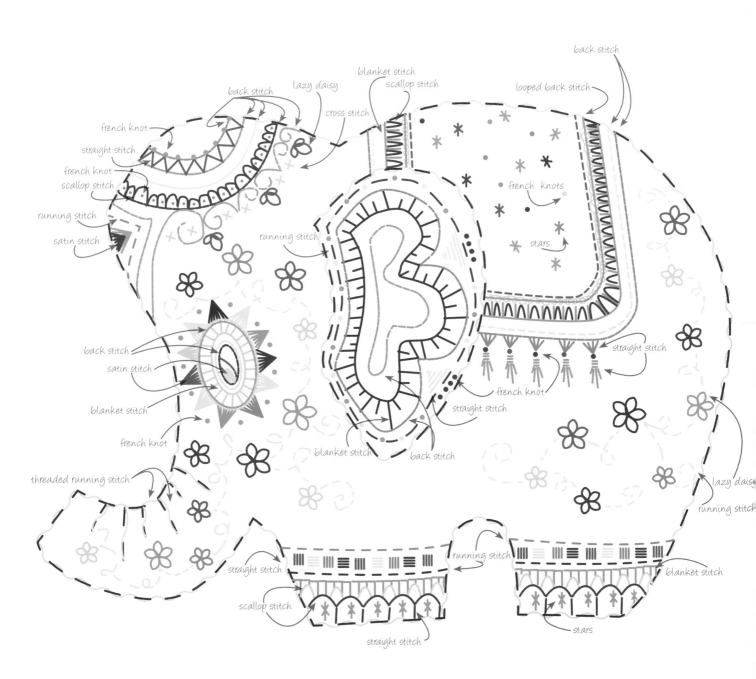

back stitch

lazy daisy

blanket stitch
scallop stitch

cross stitch

back stitch

looped back stitch

french knot

straight stitch

french knot
scallop stitch

running stitch

satin stitch

running stitch

french knots

stars

back stitch

satin stitch

blanket stitch

french knot

threaded running stitch

straight stitch

french knot

straight stitch

blanket stitch

back stitch

straight stitch

lazy daisy

running stitch

running stitch

straight stitch

scallop stitch

blanket stitch

stars

straight stitch

NELLY ALSO LOOKS GOOD USING A LIMITED PALETTE OF COLOURS OR SHADES OF ONE COLOUR

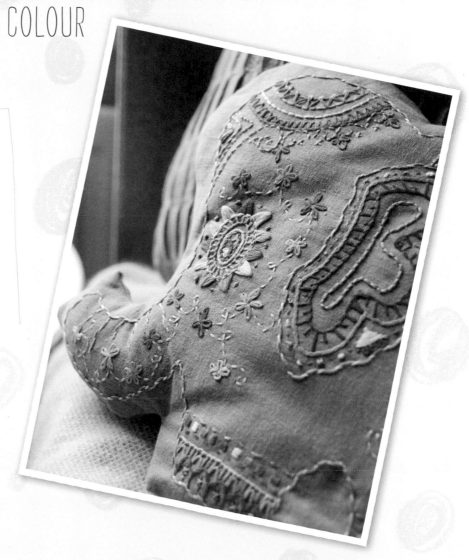

>>>

TO MAKE THE CUSHION

5. Fold the piece of lining fabric in half widthways, pin the sides together and draw around the cushion template. Machine stitch around the line, leaving a 10cm turning hole at her feet.

6. Trim away the excess fabric to leave a 1cm seam allowance. Notch the fabric at her head, trunk and around her bottom to allow the fabric to lie flat when turned. Turn inside out and press.

turning hole

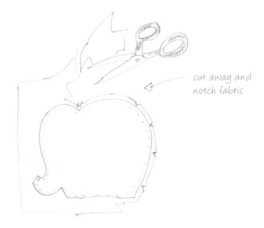

cut away and
notch fabric

7. Pin the embroidered fabric to the second linen square, embroidery facing inwards. Machine stitch around the tacked line of the elephant outline, again leaving a 10cm turning hole. Remove the tacking threads. Trim away excess fabric and notch as before. Turn right side out and press, using a damp cloth.

8. Place the lining cushion inside the outer cushion and fill with stuffing, easing it into the trunk. Hand sew the lining cushion and then the outer cushion closed. Press the seam with a damp cloth.

How to embroider ...
Blanket & scallop stitch

BLANKET STITCH
* Sew a stitch from A to B, trapping the thread under the needle.
* Put the needle back in the fabric at C and repeat step 1.

SCALLOP STITCH
* Sew a loose stitch from A to B and bring the needle up at C.
* Put the needle down at D, trapping the loose floss into a scallop.
* Bring the needle up at E to continue the row.

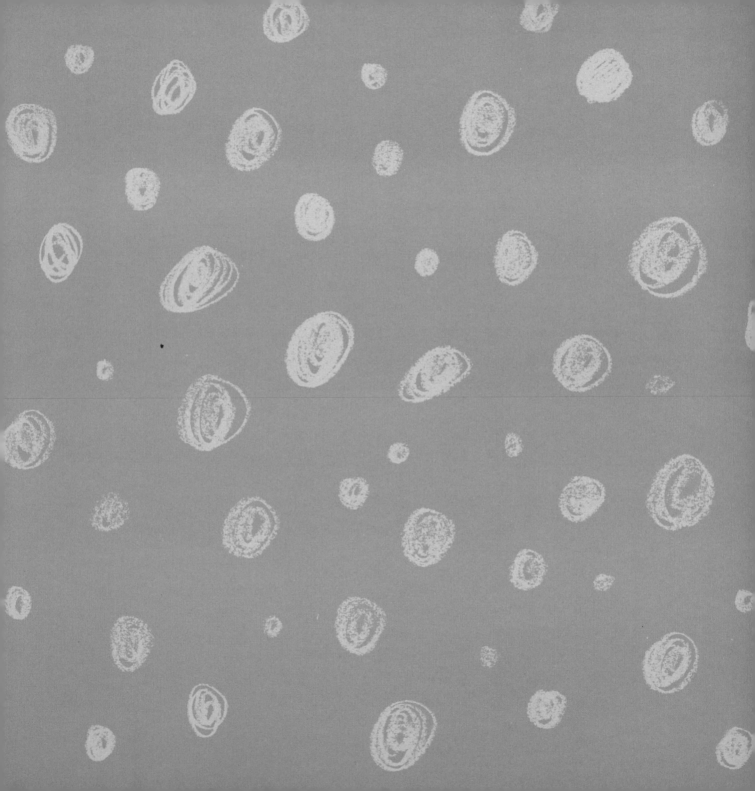

For her

* Neon flower baby doll top
* Kissing kids shoulder bag
* Hanging hearts
* Ribbon allium bag
* Little bunny book cover
* Dainty dolly bag

Neon flower baby doll top

I just love neon colours! Used cleverly, they can look really sophisticated and modern. Crisp white cotton with neon stitching makes a beautiful summer top.

For the embroidery

DMC stranded cotton embroidery thread in the following colour:

light effects neon orange E1020

10cm diameter embroidery hoop

For the top

20cm x approx 1.5m medium-weight white cotton fabric (not so thick that it is stiff and hard to sew through, but not so thin that you can see the reverse of the embroidery through it)

Tape measure

1.5m x 60cm thin white cotton

Neon sewing thread

1 wooden button, 3cm in diameter

The measurements for this project are based on your body size, so you will need to tweak them to suit your personal preferences. Try the top on at various stages to check you are happy with the length.

TO EMBROIDER THE BAND

1. To find the length of the embroidered band, first use a tape measure to measure around your body just underneath your armpits and above your breasts. Take the measurement and add 20cm – this is M1. Cut a rectangle measuring 20cm x M1 from the medium-weight cotton fabric. Fold this rectangle in half lengthways and press, then open out again.

2. Measure the distance across your chest, from one armpit to the other – this is M2. Find the middle of the fabric rectangle widthways and measure half of the M2 measurement either side of this point. This is the area for embroidery.

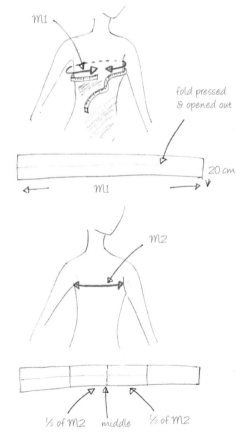

M1

fold pressed & opened out

20 cm

M1

M2

½ of M2   middle   ½ of M2

CONT. >>>

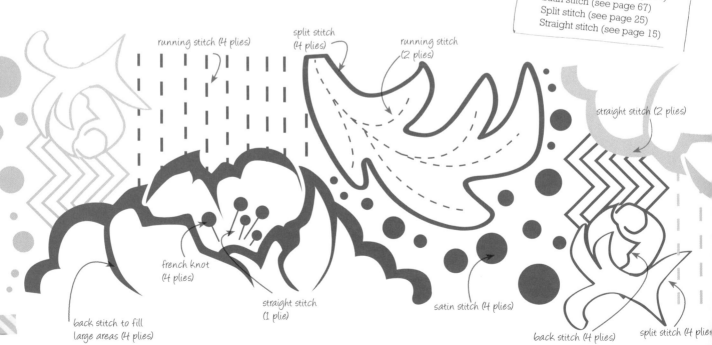

〉〉〉

3. Using a water-soluble pen, transfer the pattern below onto your fabric (see page 12). Line up the top of the embroidery with the pressed line from step 1. The grey pattern either side of the orange shows the repeat, so you need to alternately flip the pattern through 180 degrees along the length of the area to be embroidered.

4. Place the fabric in a small embroidery hoop and follow the stitch guide on the right, using one, two or four plies of floss as specified. You will need to move the embroidery hoop along as you complete each section.

5. When finished, remove from the hoop and sponge away any remaining transfer pattern; press. Turn the long raw edges inwards on both the long sides of the rectangle and press a 1cm hem. Repeat with the two short sides, then fold in half lengthways again (along the pressed line from step 1) with the embroidery on the outside.

STITCHES USED

Back stitch (see page 17)
French knots (see page 93)
Running stitch (see page 17)
Satin stitch (see page 67)
Split stitch (see page 25)
Straight stitch (see page 15)

running stitch (4 plies)

split stitch (4 plies)

running stitch (2 plies)

straight stitch (2 plies)

french knot (4 plies)

straight stitch (1 plie)

back stitch to fill large areas (4 plies)

satin stitch (4 plies)

back stitch (4 plies)

split stitch (4 plies)

TO MAKE THE BABY DOLL TOP

6. Cut a rectangle from the thin white cotton measuring 50cm x (M1 + 20cm) – so if your band is 100cm long, then the rectangle for the body of the top is 50cm x 120cm. Gather one long edge using white cotton thread. A simple way to gather Is to set your sewing machine stitch length to its longest setting, then sew two parallel rows of stitches about 5mm apart along the long edge. Find two loose ends of thread at one end of the stitch line and gently pull these. This will start gathering the fabric.

7. Continue gathering the fabric until it matches the length of your embroidered band. Even out the gathers along the length of the fabric, then insert the gathered edge inside the folded embroidered band and pin together.

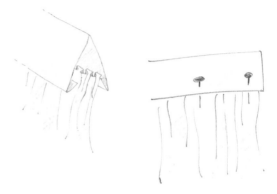

8. Carefully try on the top at this point. Wrap the top around your body so it overlaps at the front. Pin it together at the top so it is comfortable, then twist it around so the embroidered band is at the front. Adjust the gathering (it's more flattering if you have fewer gathers over your chest and under your arms).

9. If the top is too long, shorten from the bottom (be careful as cutting gathered fabric may result in a wobbly line, so mark where you want to cut, then remove the top, lay it flat and cut a straight line).

10. When you are happy with the length, turn a 5mm double hem along the two short sides and the bottom edge. Press and stitch using neon thread.

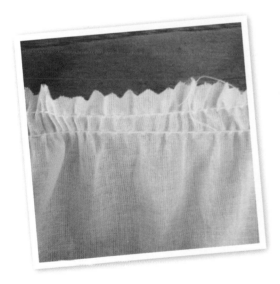

CONT. >>>

11. Using neon thread, sew the embroidered band to the gathered, hemmed body section, with a line of stitches all around the band, 5mm in from the edge.

12. The top fastens in the middle of your upper back and then just overlaps and hangs loose. Try the top on as before and fasten with a pin. (Don't tighten the top too much across your chest – allow a little room to move and breathe!) Slip the top off over your head and sew a line of stitches along where the top overlaps (see above). For decoration, sew the button firmly in place.

13. To make the straps, cut four 4 x 30cm rectangles. Take one rectangle and turn and press all raw edge inwards, so you have four neat edges. Fold in half lengthways and press. Pin together and machine stitch all around with the neon thread. Repeat with the other three straps.

14. Pop the top on again and pin the straps in place, where they feel comfortable (it may be easier to get a friend to pin the back straps in place!). Sew the straps to the inside of the top and tie in neat bows.

How to embroider ...
Fill stitches

* There are many different ways to fill large areas, firstly sew the outline of the shape using back stitch, then either ...

* Sew across the shape from left to right with alternating long and short stitches. When you've reached the other side, sew back right to left to fill the area, or
* Fill the shape with back stitch following the outline, or
* Sew straight stitches close together across the shape.

SATIN STITCH (SHOWN ON THE GREEN LEAF)
* Sew the outline of the shape with a small running stitch.
* Work straight stitches at a slight angle closely together to fill the area.
* Make sure you stitch over the outlining running stitch.

Kissing kids shoulder bag

The cute little characters on this bag were inspired by the popular Dutch Kissing Doll ornaments. However, if you want a different look, the lined bag is reversible.

SUPPLIES

For the embroidery

DMC stranded cotton embroidery thread in the following colours:

dark grey 3799, red 3801, metallic silver E677

30cm diameter embroidery hoop

For the bag

4 rectangles of mediumweight cotton fabric, each 38 x 42cm (two for the outer bag and two for the lining)

4 rectangles of fabric, 68 x 5cm, for the straps

Matching sewing thread

TO EMBROIDER THE DESIGN

1. Transfer the embroidery pattern on page 71 on to one of the rectangles of fabric (see page 12), positioning it in the centre but only 10cm up from the bottom. Place the fabric in the embroidery hoop and embroider using a full skein thickness of floss and following the stitch guide (see page 70). When finished, remove any remains of the transfer and press.

TO MAKE THE BAG

2. Pin the two rectangles for the outer bag together, right sides facing, and stitch around three sides, taking a 5mm seam allowance and leaving the top open. Repeat with the lining rectangles, also right sides facing, but this time leave the top open and a turning hole of about 15cm in the bottom seam. Snip away the excess fabric at the corners of the lining and outer bags.

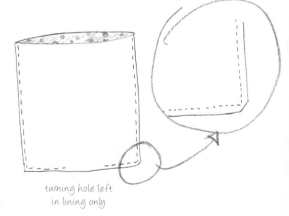

turning hole left in lining only

CONT. >>>

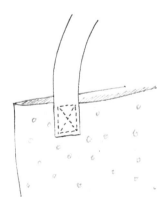

3. Turn the lining bag right side out and place inside the outer bag (which is still right sides facing). Pin the top edges together and machine stitch all around the opening.

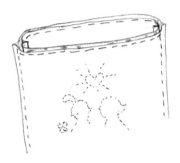

4. Push all the bag through the turning hole in the lining and rearrange it so the lining is inside the bag and the embroidered panel is on the outside. Hand stitch up the turning hole and press well.

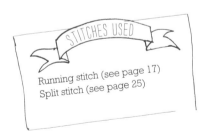

STITCHES USED

Running stitch (see page 17)
Split stitch (see page 25)

TO MAKE THE STRAPS

5. Take two of the rectangles and pin them together, right sides facing. Machine stitch all around the strap, taking a 5mm seam allowance and leaving one of the short ends open for turning. Turn right side out (if you find it tricky turning the tube, it may help to push the fabric down the tube with a pencil or knitting needle). Fold the raw edges of the open end inwards and press. Sew another seam all around the strap about 5mm in from the edge – this holds the strap flat. Repeat with the remaining two rectangles.

6. Pin about 4cm of one strap to the inside of the bag approximately 10cm in from the side. Repeat with the other end of the strap and sew in place. To strengthen, machine stitch first in a square and then stitch two diagonal lines across the square. Repeat with the second strap.

7. Decide which side of the bag you want on show today and go shopping!

Hanging hearts

These hearts are a perennial favourite and have so many uses. I hang one above my sewing machine as a pin cushion, but you could also fill them with lavender and use as a moth deterrent.

For the embroidery

DMC stranded cotton embroidery thread in the following colours:

Large heart: white, blue 996, dark blue 3838

Medium heart: white, medium grey 317, dark grey 844

Small heart: white, medium green 3347, dark green 319

For the hearts

Small pieces of fabric such as silk, calico, linen or cotton (largest piece is 15 x 30cm)

Toy stuffing

Dried lavender (optional)

Ribbon offcuts (longest piece is approx 25cm)

Small buttons for decoration

TO MAKE THE HEARTS

1. Copy your chosen heart template from page 75. Find the bias of your fabric (when the grain of your fabric runs at an angle of 45 degrees to the selvedge and the fabric stretches when you pull it). You want the bias to run diagonally across the heart as this gives it a better shape). Fold the fabric in half across the bias, right sides facing.

2. Place the template on the fabric and draw around the outline using a water-soluble pen. Pin the layers together, right sides facing, and sew around the outline, leaving a small turning hole along one straight edge.

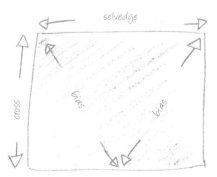

CONT. >>>

3. Cut away the excess fabric to leave a 5mm seam allowance. Make small notches at the centre of the heart's two rounded top peaks to allow the fabric to shape better and to stretch when you turn it right side out.

4. Turn the heart right side out and press. Try to press the raw edges around the turning hole inwards so you have neat edges to sew up, and gently stretch the fabric around the heart peaks.

5. Fill the heart with stuffing and dried lavender, if using, and hand stitch the hole closed.

STITCHES USED

Back stitch (see page 17)
Split stitch (see page 25)

6. Take a piece of ribbon, fold in half and pin the two raw ends to the reverse of the heart. Hand stitch in place on the back of the heart, all the way through the heart and back again. Sew a button to the front of the heart to cover up the stitches.

TO EMBROIDER THE DESIGNS

7. The geometric patterns are easy to draw freehand on to the hearts using a water-soluble pen. For the semi-circles and chevrons, start at the bottom of the heart and work upwards. For the straight lines, draw lines radiating out from the button. Follow the embroidery pattern for guidance.

8. Embroider all the lines of one colour at a time, using four plies of floss. You can push the needle through the stuffing to get to the next place you need to embroider. Try to embroider only on the front of the heart – don't push your needle all the way through to the other side.

split stitch

back stitch

split stitch

Ribbon allium bag

As a change from using floss, this bag is embroidered using different widths and types of ribbon and a selection of beads. The same repertoire of embroidery stitches is used, but with a few differences (see page 81).

For the embroidery

20cm diameter embroidery hoop

Eight 2m lengths of ribbon, in widths from 3mm to 1cm

Needles with holes large enough for the ribbons to fit through

Matching embroidery threads

Small beads in a variety of shades

For the bag

1m x 50cm mediumweight fabric

1m x 50cm cotton for lining

Pair of D-shaped wooden handles

Back stitch (see page 17)
French knots (see page 93)
Lazy daisy (see page 87)
Running stitch (see page 17)
Stars (see page 53)
Straight stitch (see page 15)

TO EMBROIDER THE DESIGN

1. Enlarge the bag and gusset templates from pages 125–126 by 200%. Cut out and pin the bag template to the bag fabric. Draw around using tailor's chalk or a water-soluble pen.

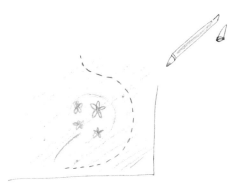

2. Tack the outline using close, even length stitches so you can see the shape of the bag on both sides of the fabric.

3. Copy the allium pattern overleaf on to the fabric using tailor's carbon paper (see page 13) or, if the fabric is thin and pale, you may be able to trace it. You don't have to copy every single flower and star onto your fabric – you can just draw the larger flowers and then fill in the gaps when embroidering.

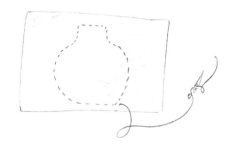

CONT >>>

4. If your fabric is textured, draw the pattern freehand using a water-soluble pen or tailor's chalk. Draw around a saucer 14cm in diameter for the large allium and a 7cm one for the smaller one. Draw the largest flowers as a guide and fill in the rest when embroidering. Don't forget to draw the stalks.

5. Place the fabric in the embroidery hoop, then follow the stitch guides on pages 76, 77 and 79 to embroider the ribbon flowers, using a mixture of ribbon colours and widths. Use a full thickness of embroidery thread to sew small lazy daisies and stars to fill in the spaces between flowers.

6. Create sparkly centres for the flowers by sewing three or four beads into the middle of the flowers. Sew the beads on using a similar coloured sewing thread and a couple of stitches through each bead to hold them securely in place.

TO MAKE THE BAG LINING

7. Place the bag template on to the lining fabric. Trace around the template and cut out, adding a 1cm seam allowance all around. You will need two pieces.

8. Cut out one gusset piece using the template. Fold the rectangle over to the wrong side by 1cm at each short end and press.

9. Starting at point A, pin one of the bag pieces to the gusset around the bottom to point B, then tack in place. Machine stitch, leaving a 15cm turning gap at the base of the bag (leave the tacking stitches in place). Repeat with the other bag side, but don't leave a turning gap. Keep the bag turned inside out.

back stitch

long running stitch

CONT. 》》》

KEY

star flower

daisy

simple flower

french knot

beads

star 1

star 2

stars

daisy

star flower

beads

straight stitch

french knot

EXTRA

These embroidered alliums also look great on cushion covers (make your own or customise existing ones) or on the tea cosy on page 21.

》》》

TO ASSEMBLE THE BAG

10. Trim the embroidered fabric to within 1cm of the tacked outline. Repeat step 7 to make a second bag piece. Repeat step 8 for the gusset in the main fabric. Make up the outer bag following step 9, but don't leave a turning gap. Make sure you position the front piece so the embroidery will face outwards. Press the seams of the bag and turn right side out.

11. Place the embroidered bag inside the lining bag (which is inside out) so the embroidery is hidden between the inner and outer bag and the lining bag is on the outside. (When turned right way out, the seams will be hidden inside the bag.)

12. Tack the raw edges of the bag top together on both sides, making sure the tops of the inner and outer gussets line up. Machine stitch around both sides, leaving the top open (for the handles).

13. Turn the bag right side out through the turning gap and push the lining into the outer bag. Hand stitch the turning gap closed.

14. Tidy up the short sides of the gusset by turning the raw edges inwards, press and then hand stitch the lining and bag together.

15. To attach the handles, turn the raw edges of the bag and lining inwards and press. Wrap the bag around each handle, pin and sew in place. Try to get your machine needle as close to the bag handle as possible. Repeat on the second handle.

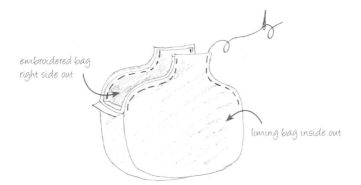

embroidered bag
right side out

lining bag inside out

STAR FLOWER
* Bring the needle up through the fabric at A.
* Push the needle back into the fabric at B through the centre of the ribbon.
* Don't pull the needle too hard or it will pull the ribbon through the fabric too.
* Bring the needle back up at A and repeat.

DAISY
* Sew a loop by taking the needle up and down at A and B.
* Bring the needle back out at C, then in at D securing the loop of ribbon in place.
* Bring the needle back up at A and repeat for more petals.

How to embroider ...
Ribbon flowers

SIMPLE FLOWER
* Bring the needle up at A, back down at B and up again at A. Repeat.

Little bunny book cover

This sweet fabric book cover is a nifty way to jazz up a boring notebook (or to disguise a book you may not want to be caught reading on the bus!).

For the embroidery

DMC stranded cotton embroidery thread in the following colours:

White (shown in grey on the stitch guide), beige 842, baby pink 819, baby blue 3325, avocado green 470, pale yellow 744, tangerine 741, raspberry 3832, brown 610, dark grey 413

20cm diameter embroidery hoop

For the book cover

Tape measure

Linen, calico or cotton, 50 x 24cm (for an A5-sized book; see step 1 for other book sizes)

20cm length of ribbon, 5mm wide (optional)

TO CUT THE FABRIC

1. If your book is not A5 sized, work out the dimension of the piece of fabric you need. First, measure the height of the front cover and add 1.5cm to both the top and bottom. Using a tape measure, measure the closed book from the outer edge of the front cover, around the spine and across to the outer edge of the back cover. Add half the width of the covers again for the flaps, plus 1.5cm to each end. Cut the fabric to this size.

measure

Tulip

lazy daisy

back stitch

straight stitch

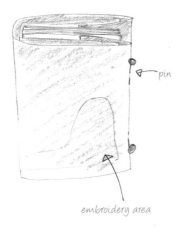

pin

embroidery area

2. Wrap your book in the fabric and close the cover. This will make creases for the front and back flaps and give you an indication of where to draw the embroidery pattern. Mark the creases with pins.

TO EMBROIDER THE DESIGN

3. Transfer the pattern to the fabric (see page 12). Place the fabric in the embroidery hoop and embroider following the stitch guide. When finished, remove any traces of the embroidery pattern and press. Use four plies for the main bunnies and flowers and two plies for their eyes and whiskers.

split stitch

straight stitch
(2 plies)

split stitch

tulips

running stitch

TO MAKE UP THE COVER

4. Wrap the book in the fabric jacket again to check the flap creases.

5. Turn each edge of the material over twice to make a double hem (your turns should only be about 5mm per turn). Press.

6. Machine stitch the hems of the two short edges. Fold the two flaps inwards and pin in place (the right side of the embroidery should be on the opposite side to the flaps). Machine stitch along the top and bottom edges of the cover.

7. Trim off all stray threads and press. To fit the cover onto the notebook, carefully fold the book's front and back covers backwards (towards the spine) and place one cover into each of the fabric flaps, then close.

8. If you wish to make a bookmark, hand sew the length of ribbon onto the book jacket at the spine.

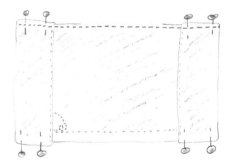

LAZY DAISY
* Sew a loose stitch from A to B, bringing the needle up at C.
* Bring the needle back down at D over the loop fixing it in place.
* Bring the needle up at E and repeat for more petals.

How to embroider ...
Flowers

TULIPS
* Sew a short stem using back stitch.
* Make two leaves by sewing a single lazy daisy petal for each leaf.
* Make a wide lazy daisy petal, then a second narrower one inside.
* Finish with a straight stitch.

Dainty dolly bag

This little drawstring bag is useful for storing all manner of things, from jewellery to lingerie. Embroidering the motif on a separate smaller piece of fabric makes it much easier to place in the embroidery hoop

For the embroidery

30 x 30cm piece of white cotton fabric

16cm diameter embroidery hoop

DMC stranded embroidery thread in the following colours:

pink 3708, white, metallic light gold E677, light gold 677, dark brown 3371, mid pink 5351, pale peach 353, pale blue 519, blue 518, dark grey 310

10cm length of lacy ribbon, 1.5cm wide, for the dress

5 star-shaped sequins

10 round sequins

For the bag

68 x 30cm piece of cotton fabric

Bondaweb

2m length of ribbon, approx 2cm wide, for the drawstring

Pinking shears

TO EMBROIDER THE DESIGN

1. Transfer the embroidery design from page 91 on to the fabric using a water-soluble pen (see page 12). Place the fabric in the hoop and embroider, following the instructions to the right and the pattern on page 91. (The running stitch border is not stitched until you reach step 3.)

TO ATTACH THE EMBROIDERY TO THE BAG

2. Cut a piece of Bondaweb slightly larger than the oval of the design, then iron it on to the reverse side of the fabric following the manufacturer's instructions. Using pinking shears, cut out the oval shape, then iron onto the bag.

3. For a decorative edge, embroider around the oval with a small running stitch.

* **For her body, dress and necklace**, use four plies of floss.
* **For her hair**, use two plies of normal floss and two plies of metallic floss. This makes it easier to sew as metallic thread has a tendency to snag.
* **For the stars**, use a single plie of thread for a dainty decoration.
* **For her face**, use two plies of floss for her eyes and a single plie for her nose and four plies for her mouth.
* **For the decoration**, sew a running stitch along one long edge of the ribbon and gather slightly so it is the same length as the top of her dress. Knot each end of the thread. Sew into place using two plies of floss, adding the round sequins in as you go.
* **For the tiara**, sew the star-shaped sequins on to her hair using a similar coloured thread.

CONT. >>>

TO MAKE THE BAG

4. Fold the fabric in half, short end to short end and right side out. Pin and machine stitch the front and back of the bag together along each side, about 5mm in. Leave a 2cm opening on each side 4cm down from the top.

5. Turn the bag inside out and sew another seam line 1cm in from the edge, make sure you sew far enough in that you cover all the rough edges of the material (that will be on the other side of the bag).

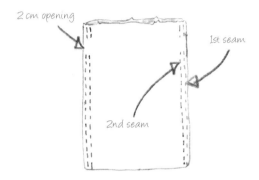

2 cm opening

1st seam

2nd seam

6. Turn and press a 5mm hem along the open top edge, then turn over approximately 3cm – the holes left for the drawstring ribbon should be close to the top of the bag on the outside. Machine stitch all around the top of the bag, close to the bottom edge of the turnover, to create the channel for the drawstring, turn right side out and press.

7. Cut the ribbon in half. Attach a safety pin to 1m of ribbon, pass it through one hole and then use the safety pin to pull the ribbon all the way around the bag and out the same hole. Repeat with the other ribbon and the other hole. Trim the ends of the ribbon into a 'V' shape to prevent fraying.

CONT.)))

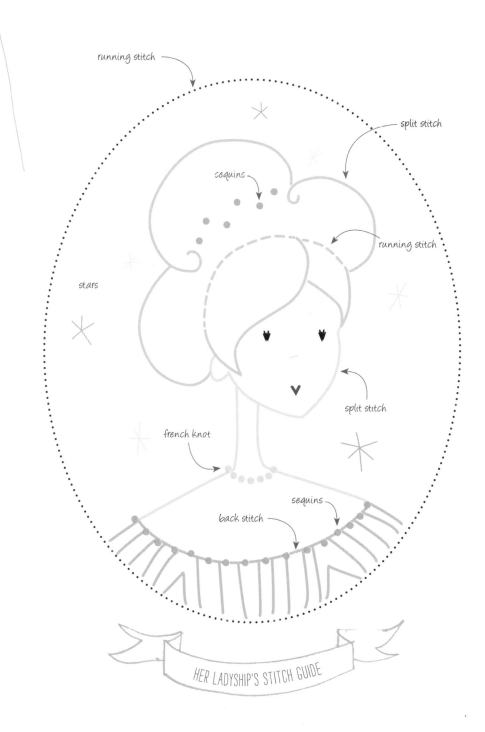

STITCHES USED

Back stitch (see page 17)
Eyes (see page 93)
French knot (see page 93)
Running stitch (see page 17)
Split stitch (see page 25)
Stars (see page 53)

running stitch

split stitch

sequins

running stitch

stars

split stitch

french knot

sequins

back stitch

HER LADYSHIP'S STITCH GUIDE

PERSONALISE THIS DOLLY BAG
            WITH THE NAME OF YOUR
OWN LITTLE PRINCESS!

PRINCESS PEACH

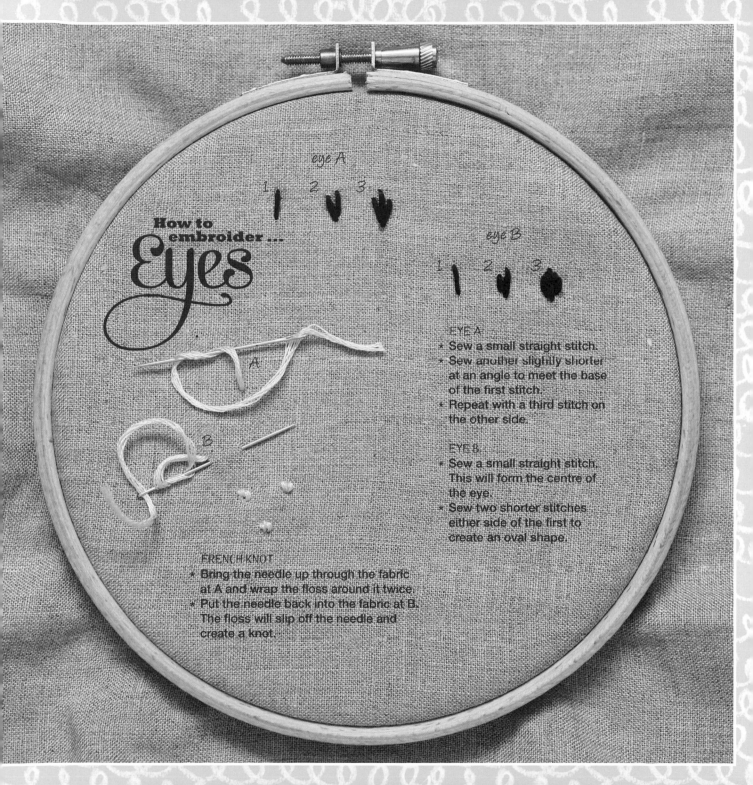

How to embroider ...
Eyes

eye A

1 2 3

eye B

1 2 3

A

B

EYE A
* Sew a small straight stitch.
* Sew another slightly shorter at an angle to meet the base of the first stitch.
* Repeat with a third stitch on the other side.

EYE B
* Sew a small straight stitch. This will form the centre of the eye.
* Sew two shorter stitches either side of the first to create an oval shape.

FRENCH KNOT
* Bring the needle up through the fabric at A and wrap the floss around it twice.
* Put the needle back into the fabric at B. The floss will slip off the needle and create a knot.

For children

* Children's keepsake samplers
* Party gift bags
* Counting sheep pillow
* Alphabet wall hanging

Children's keepsake samplers

The three samplers shown here are a modern version of traditional sampler embroideries, taking children's drawings and immortalising them in stitch.

For the embroidery

Embroidery hoops – I've used three with diameters of 22cm, 18cm and 12cm (these double up as the frames)

Embroidery threads in the colours of your choice

For the samplers

Squares of coloured cotton or material linen, 10cm larger than your embroidery hoop

3cm wide Washi tape (a type of pretty coloured and patterned masking tape) or paint and paintbrush

TO EMBROIDER THE DESIGNS

1. I have used three drawings by my nephews, Oliver and Elliot. I transferred them onto the fabric by tracing them with a water-soluble pen (see page 12), but you could ask your child to draw directly onto the fabric when it is placed in the embroidery hoop. Embroider the drawing using whichever colours and stitches you like and add their name and age or birth date. Use four plies of thread.

2. Remove the fabric from the embroidery hoop. Carefully sponge away the pattern and press.

TO FRAME THE SAMPLERS

3. If you would like to have a coloured frame, cover the outer frame of the embroidery hoop with Washi tape. It is easiest to do this using short 10cm lengths of tape – lie them lengthways around the frame and fold the excess tape down over the sides. If painting, allow the paint to dry thoroughly.

4. Place the embroidery back in the embroidery hoop, stretch it well, then trim away excess fabric, leaving about 1.5cm all around. Snip this excess fabric at 2cm intervals towards the hoop. Turn the hoop over and run a strip of double-sided tape or a thin layer of fabric glue around the inside of the hoop. Fold the excess fabric onto the sticky strip or glue and press in place with your fingers.

Originally samplers were made by women and children to learn and practise their embroidery stitches. They often commemorated special occasions such as births or marriages.

Party gift bags

These are top-of-the-range party bags! You could also use them instead of wrapping paper or pack them full of little treats for the lucky recipient's birthday breakfast – like a birthday stocking!

SUPPLIES

For the embroidery

DMC stranded cotton embroidery thread in the following colours:

For a girl: orange 721, pinky red 892, purple 996, bright blue 333, pale pink 819, lime 907

For a boy: bright blue 333, purple 996, reddy pink 892, grey 310, yellow 307, dark beige 950, orange 721

For the balloons: beige 3770, pink 605, reddy pink 892, purple 996, bright blue 333

14cm diameter embroidery hoop

For each bag

50 x 35cm rectangle of cotton fabric

50 x 35cm rectangle iron-on stiffening

Pencil and ruler

15 x 4cm piece of cardboard

Pinking shears

TO EMBROIDER THE DESIGN

1. Enlarge the template on page 120 by 250% (although you could make these bags to any size you wish). Place the rectangle of fabric on the template and mark the embroidery area with a water-soluble pen. Transfer your chosen pattern from page 100 on to the fabric (see page 12). Embroider using a whole skein thickness of floss and following the embroidery guide overleaf. When complete, sponge away any excess pattern lines and press.

TO MAKE THE BAG

2. Using a ruler and pencil trace the bag template onto the rectangle of stiffener. Following the manufacturer's instructions, place the stiffener on the reverse side of the fabric and iron the two rectangles together. This will stiffen the fabric and allow the bag to stand upright when complete.

3. To create the sides of the bag, place the fabric flat on the table, embroidered side facing up. Fold concertina-style along the drawn lines in the following way: from the left-hand side, first line inwards, second line out, third line in. Repeat on the right-hand side. The two short edges should join up now with a 1cm overlap. Also fold the long bottom edge upwards. This folding creases the bag's sides and makes it easier to form after you have sewn it together.

CONT. >>>

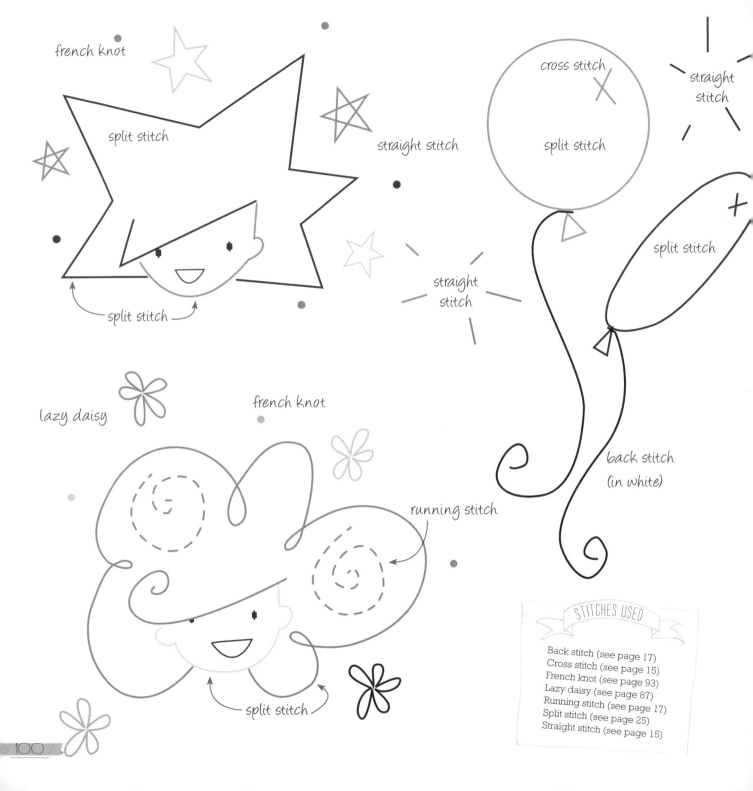

french knot

split stitch

split stitch

split stitch

straight stitch

cross stitch

split stitch

straight stitch

straight stitch

split stitch

back stitch (in white)

lazy daisy

french knot

running stitch

split stitch

STITCHES USED

Back stitch (see page 17)
Cross stitch (see page 15)
French knot (see page 93)
Lazy daisy (see page 87)
Running stitch (see page 17)
Split stitch (see page 25)
Straight stitch (see page 15)

4. Unfold and place the two short sides of the bag together, right sides facing. Pin and machine stitch, taking a 5mm seam allowance, to form a tube. Next, fold flat with the seam in the middle. Pin the bottom of the tube together and machine stitch the base. This creates your basic bag.

5. Turn the bag right side out. The pre-creased lines should now fold in on themselves, forming gussets at both sides, and the bottom should form a flat base with a little wing on either side.

6. Squash the bag flat with your hands – the little wing should fold in half and create a triangle shape in the gusset. Tuck the wing inside itself so it lies flat on the base (this may require a little wiggling!). Press.

7. Place the piece of cardboard in the bottom of the bag to give it a stable base (cut it to fit if necessary), then trim the top of the bag with pinking shears and fill with goodies.

Counting sheep pillow

This colourful pillowcase with traditional Oxford edges and embroidered with dancing sheep will help the little ones drift off to sleep with happy dreams.

For the embroidery

DMC stranded embroidery thread in the following colours:

white, orange 741, olive green 907, mid pink 3708, lilac 340, lemon yellow 727, mid orange 972, gunmetal grey 169, satin blue S800

18cm diameter embroidery hoop

For the pillow

120 x 74cm piece of white cotton or flannel (not too thin or the reverse of the embroidery thread will show through)

57 x 35cm children's pillow

TO EMBROIDER THE COVER

1. Turn a double hem of 1cm on the short edges of the fabric, turning the hem to the reverse side of the fabric. Hem the two short sides (these will be the opening for the pillowcase, which will be on the back).

2. To find the area to be embroidered, fold the fabric in half, short edge to short edge, and make a mark on each side at the fold. Open the fabric out again, place right side up and measure 18cm from these marks in each direction. Using a water-soluble pen, draw a line across the fabric top and bottom (A and B). Measure 8cm in from each outer edge and draw another line. This rectangle is the area to embroider.

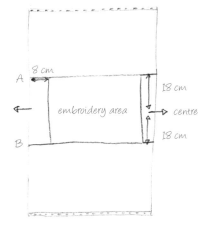

CONT. >>>

star

long running stitch

satin stitch

C

split stitch

back stitch

D

satin stitch

star

long running stitch

long running stitch

star

star

lazy daisy

split stitch

A

french knots

B

tulip

back stitch

satin stitch

3. Using a water-soluble pen (see page 12), trace the sheep from pages 104–105 on to the front of the fabric wherever you like or follow my layout below (I have kept the centre of the pillowcase empty so it is more comfortable for little heads to rest on). Once the sheep are in place, add the stars and spin lines to complete the design.

4. Place the fabric in the embroidery hoop. Following the stitch guide on pages 104–105, embroider the design using a whole skein thickness of floss. You will have to move the fabric around in the hoop to complete the design. It's easier if you embroider a whole sheep at a time rather than having the design cut off by the edge of the hoop. If your fabric is quite thin, try to be neat with the back of your embroidery as stray threads will show through.

TO MAKE THE PILLOW CASE

5. Lay the fabric flat, with the embroidery facing up. Fold the two shorter ends of the fabric inwards at lines A and B. This will allow the fabric to overlap by about 10cm. Press these folds and pin.

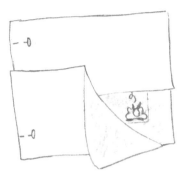

this is the layout of the sheep on my pillow

EXTRA!

These little sheep designs would look great on the Dainty Dolly Bag on page 88 or the Woodland Storage Boxes on page 34. Alternatively, make a matching hot water bottle cover on page 48.

6. Machine stitch along the two short sides, taking a 1cm seam allowance. Remove the pins and turn the case right side out. Press to finish, using a pressing cloth to protect the embroidery.

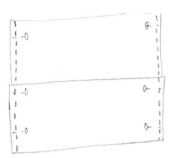

8. Carefully rinse the pillowcase to remove all the pen marks, dry and press. Insert the pillow and keep your fingers crossed for a quiet night's sleep!

7. To sew the Oxford edging, measure 7cm in from the top and bottom of the case and draw a line, these lines and the two lines drawn previous will be your guides for sewing the edges. Pin the layers of fabric together and pin the opening closed so that it doesn't move. Machine stitch a rectangle of stitches around your drawn lines.

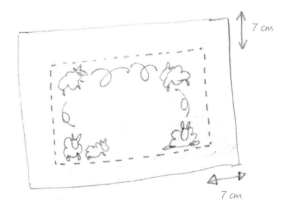

7 cm

7 cm

Alphabet wall hanging

The letter designs for this sampler are so versatile. If you don't want to make the complete wall hanging, choose some letters and embroider them wherever you like – as monograms on clothes or bags, or as cute slogans on cushions and book covers.

For the embroidery

DMC stranded cotton embroidery thread (see page 111 for colours)

Small embroidery hoop (approx 10cm in diameter)

For the wall hanging

28 squares of linen in various colours, 15 x 15cm

1m x 60cm linen or cotton for backing

5 rectangles of linen for tabs, 6 x 10cm

Matching sewing thread

9 pompoms, 5cm in diameter

60cm ribbon or cord for hanging

60cm length of dowel, 1.5cm in diameter

Spray paint or acrylic paint

Drill

TO EMBROIDER THE DESIGN

1. Transfer the letters and illustrations from pages 112–116 to your fabric squares (see page 12), positioning them centrally. Place in the embroidery hoop and embroider as per the stitch guides, using two plies of floss. When complete, remove any visible transfer marks and press.

TO MAKE THE WALL HANGING

2. On the reverse of each square, draw a seam line 1cm in from the edge on all four sides, using a water-soluble pen. Place the letter B face up on a table. Place letter A on top of B face down (so the neat sides of the embroideries are touching and making sure they are both pointing in the same direction). Pin along the drawn seam line and machine stitch together, following the drawn line. Open up and press flat.

3. Repeat with letters C and D, placing D on the table and C on top, face down. Pin and sew along the left-hand side. Open up and press flat.

4. Place the CD rectangle on the table face up and place the AB rectangle on top face down. Pin and sew along the left-hand side. Open up and press flat. This has created your first row.

CONT. >>>

5. Repeat with the six other rows, checking that they all face in the right direction.

6. When you have seven rows each of four squares, place the ABCD row on the table face up and place the EFGH rectangle on top, face down but rotated 180 degrees. (You want to sew the bottom of the ABCD row to the top of the EFGH row.) Pin together and machine stitch along the bottom edge.

7. Repeat with the rest of the rows. Again, make sure that they all face in the right direction. Press well.

8. Make the hanging tabs by folding each 6 x 10cm rectangle in half lengthways, right sides facing, and sew down the long raw edges. Turn each right side out and press so the seam is in the middle of the tube. Fold in half widthways to make a loop and pin to the right side of the sampler with the majority of the tab laying on the embroidered letters and the folded edge facing towards the base of the hanging. Pin one tab at each end, one in the middle and the remaining two evenly spaced between them.

9. Place the backing fabric on top of the letters and tabs, right sides facing, and pin all around. Machine stitch 1cm in from the edge (make sure you sew far enough in to catch all the edges of the squares). Leave a turning hole along the bottom edge.

10. Trim away any excess fabric cutting the corners on the diagonal to make the hanging less bulky at the corners, remove the pins and turn right side out. The tabs will pop out along the top. Hand stitch the turning hole closed and press well.

11. Hand stitch the row of pompoms to the bottom of the hanging.

TO HANG THE HANGING

12. Paint the dowel with spray or acrylic paint and allow to dry thoroughly. Drill a hole vertically through the dowel 2cm in from each end. Thread one end of the ribbon through one hole and tie a knot. Thread the dowel through the tabs, then thread the other end of the ribbon through the other hole and tie a knot to secure. Your embroidery is now ready to hang.

CONT. 〉〉〉

Letter colour chart

A
mid orange 742
lemon yellow 3078
gold 3852
dark orange 740

B
pale pink 818
white
turquoise 813

C
lime green 907
turquoise 813
sage 3364
metallic blue E316

D
white
lemon yellow 3078
mid orange 742
mid yellow 972

E
pink 962
pale bronze E677

F
purple 340
metallic blue E334
dark blue 996
dark purple 3835

G
white
grey 317
mid yellow 972
lime green 907

H
brown
red 309
dark pink 321
dark green 700
pale bronze E677

I
dark pink 321
pink 760
yellow 743

J
blue 996
dark blue 824
white
yellow 792
lemon yellow 3078
mid orange 742

K
white
pink 761
pale pink 818
beige 842
pale green 3819

L
lemon yellow 3078
mid yellow 972
white
pink 602

M
light blue 747
pale lilac 341
pale pink 818

N
purple 340
dark purple 3835
lime 907
peach 353
pink 760

O
blue 996
white
dark blue 824
metallic blue E334

P
pink 760
dark pink 321
light pink 3706
pale pink 818
metallic pink E316

Q
orange 740
silver E168
light orange 742
pale blue 747
yellow 743

R
dark pink 321
pink 3706

S
lemon yellow 3078
yellow 743
gold 3852

T
lime green 907
pea green 702
brown 3371
lemon yellow 3078

U
turquoise 813
dark blue 824
pink 962
peach 353

V
lemon yellow 3078
gold 3852

W
red 309
pale pink 818
pale blue 747

X
dark orange 740
mid orange 742
dark pink 321
pale pink 818

Y
dark blue 996
white
pink 818

Z
pink 818

HEART
dark pink 321
white
grey 762
gold 3852

BLUEBIRD
lime 907
pink 818
dark pink 321
blue 996
turquoise 813
yellow 3078

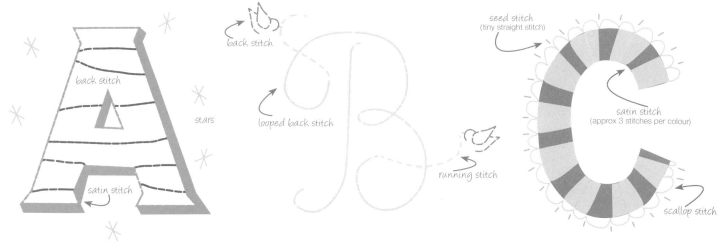

back stitch

looped back stitch

running stitch

back stitch

stars

satin stitch

seed stitch
(tiny straight stitch)

satin stitch
(approx 3 stitches per colour)

scallop stitch

Templates and stitch guides shown at 100%

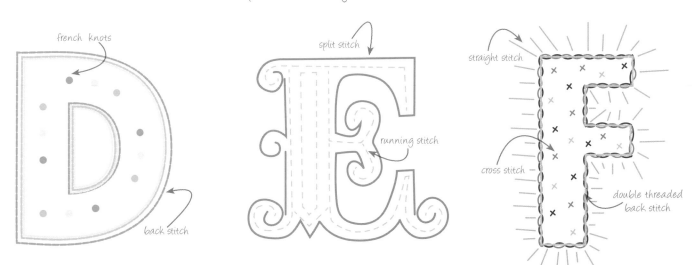

french knots

back stitch

split stitch

running stitch

straight stitch

cross stitch

double threaded
back stitch

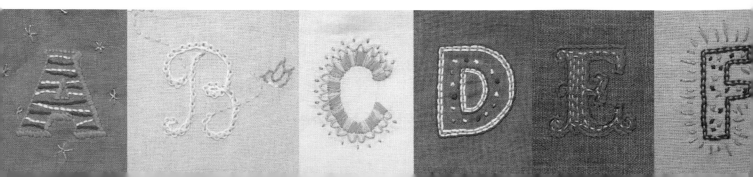

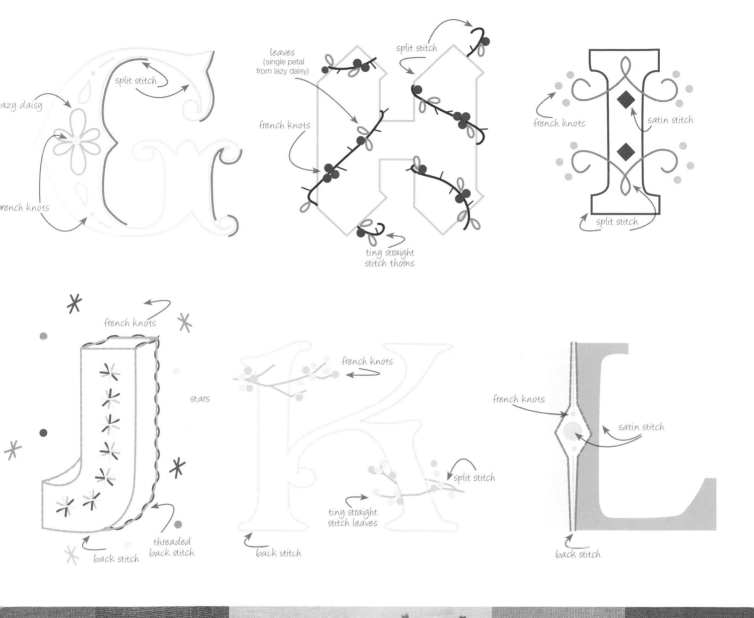

lazy daisy

split stitch

french knots

leaves
(single petal
from lazy daisy)

split stitch

french knots

tiny straight
stitch thorns

french knots

satin stitch

split stitch

french knots

stars

french knots

french knots

satin stitch

split stitch

tiny straight
stitch leaves

threaded
back stitch

back stitch

back stitch

back stitch

double threaded two-colour running stitch

lazy daisy

threaded back stitch

french knots

back stitch

two-colour running stitch

split stitch

stars

back stitch

multi coloured fill stitch

(sew straight stitches in each colour to fill the letter outline)

tulips

straight stitches to a point

split stitch

threaded back stitch

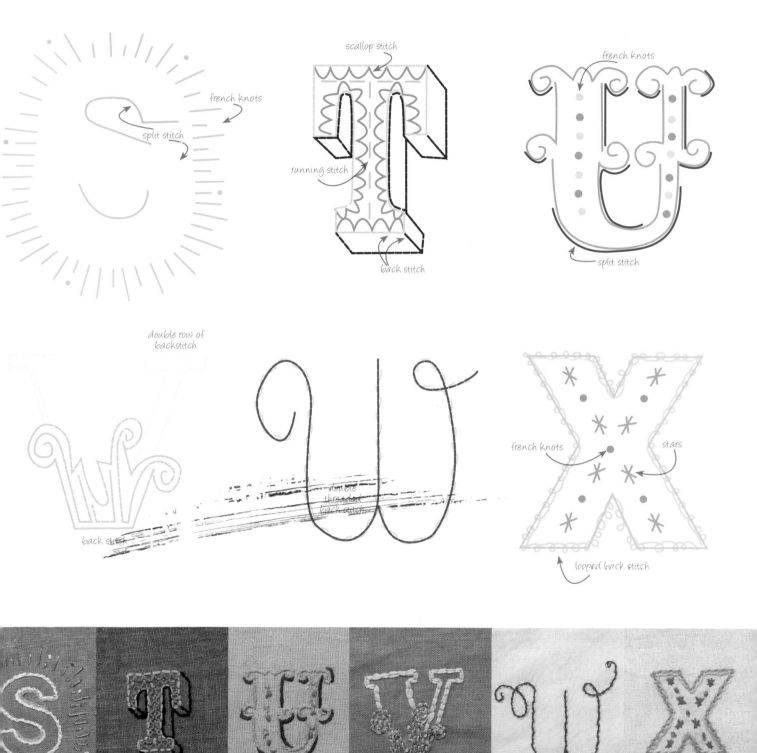

french knots

split stitch

scallop stitch

running stitch

back stitch

french knots

split stitch

double row of
backstitch

back stitch

double
threaded
back stitch

french knots

stars

looped back stitch

back stitch

satin stitch

EXTRA!

Use the banner space on the heart motif to personalise your work with either your name or the date.

satin stitch

back stitch

lazy daisy

french knot

split stitch

straight stitch

THIS HANGING IS A GREAT
WAY FOR CHILDREN TO
LEARN THE ALPHABET!

The templates

Party gift bags

(see page 98)

This template is shown
reduced to 40%, so enlarge
it on a photocopier by 250%.

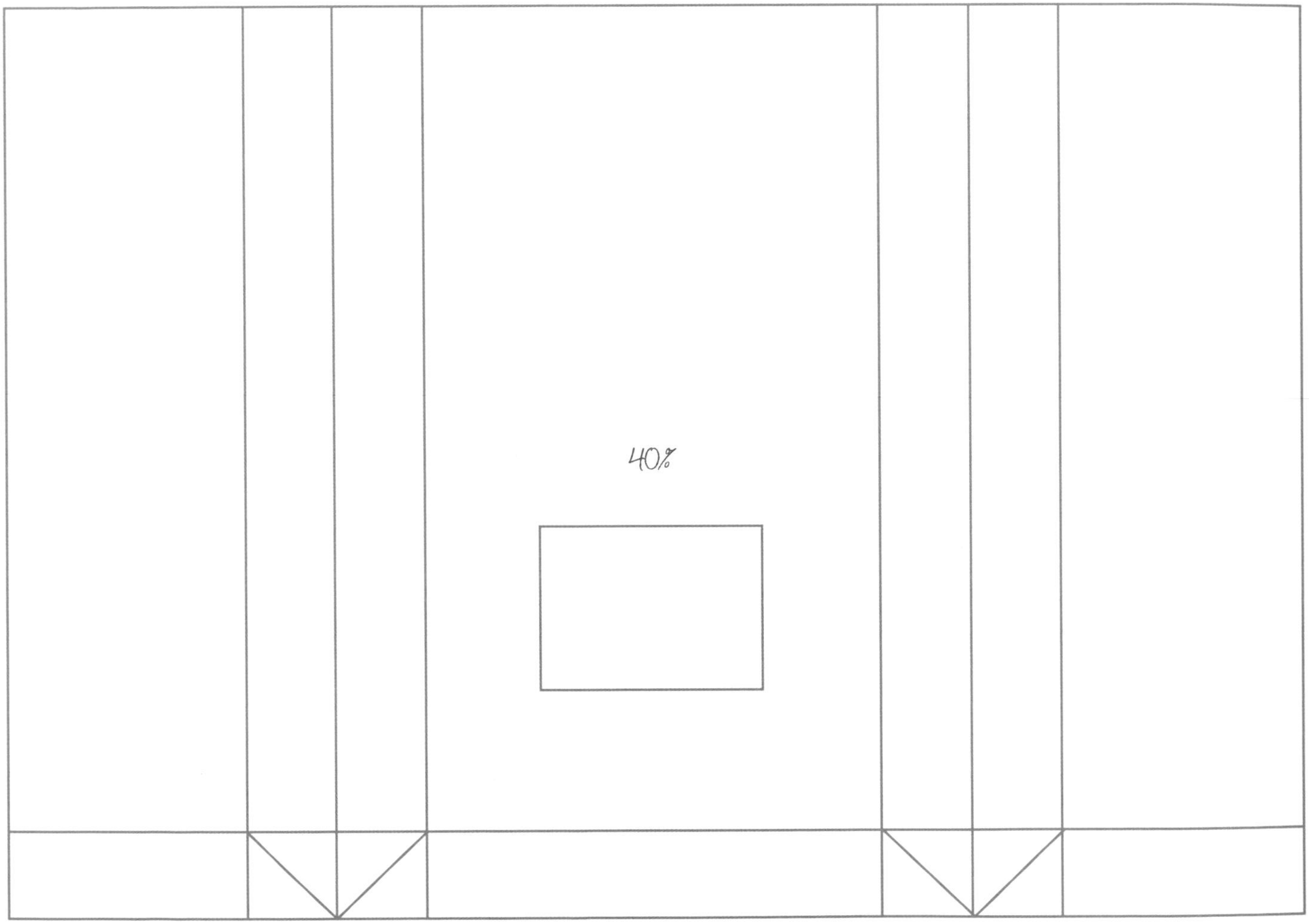

40%

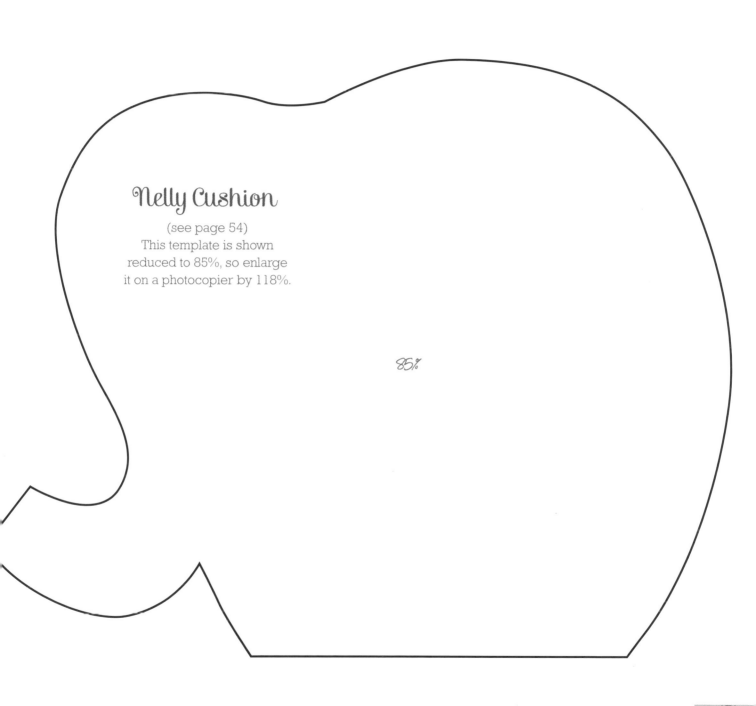

Nelly Cushion

(see page 54)
This template is shown
reduced to 85%, so enlarge
it on a photocopier by 118%.

85%

100%

Bird cage tea cosy

(see page 21)
Trace and use at this size.

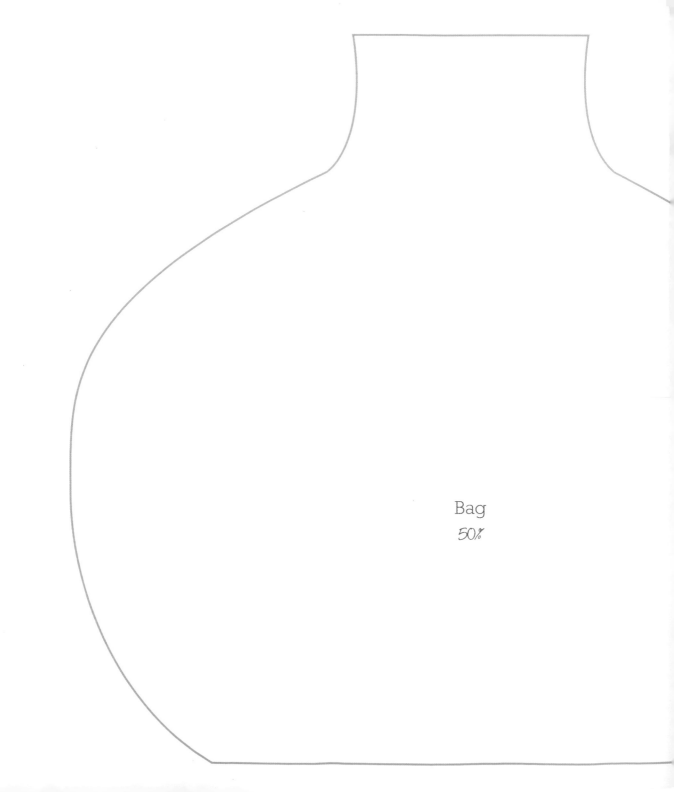

Bag
50%

50%

double length

Bag gusset

Ribbon allium bag

(see page 76)
The bag shape and gusset are both shown
reduced to 50%, so enlarge them by 200%
on a photocopier.

Resources

WHERE TO GET IT

EMBROIDERY RESOURCES

DMC Creative World
A lovely online resource for DMC flosses with online tutorials and free patterns.
www.dmccreative.co.uk
Tel: 0116 275 4000
This DMC website gives the actual colours of the yarns.
www.dmc-usa.com/Conversion-Charts.aspx

Sew and So
The UK's largest online needlecraft shop. A wonderful array of flosses, needles and everything you'll need to get you started.
www.sewandso.co.uk
Tel: 0800 013 0150

Yarntree
If you can't get hold of DMC flosses, this website tells you the Anchor variation.
www.yarntree.com/019dmccn.htm

FABRIC AND HABERDASHERY

Barnett Lawson
Wholesaler open to the public. Brilliant for large amounts of trimmings, but also sells some by the meter.
16–17 Little Portland Street
London W1W 8NE
Tel: 020 7636 8591
www.bltrimmings.com

Fabric Rehab
Lovely fabrics for patchwork and other projects. Lots of cute Japanese designs.
www.fabricrehab.co.uk

Eclectic Maker
Fabulous fabrics and sewing supplies.
T: 0845 862 5552
www.eclecticmaker.co.uk

Hobbycraft
A nationwide hobby and craft superstore. Just brilliant.
Tel: 01202 596100
www.hobbycraft.co.uk

Jane Means
Jane sells a plethora of ribbons at her online store and also offers gift-wrapping courses.
Tel: 01522 522 544
www.janemeans.com

Craftability
An Aladdin's cave of sewing/craft supplies.
4 St Lawrence Street
Ipswich IP1 1DN
Tel: 01473 257 550
www.craftability-ipswich.co.uk

The Stitchery
A great haberdashers.
12–16 Riverside
Cliffe Bridge
High Street
Lewes
East Sussex BN7 2RE
Tel: 01273 473 577
www.the-stitchery.co.uk

Bag Clasps
An online store that has pretty much every single type of bag handle you could wish for, including the ones used in the Allium bag.
Tel: 07990 960 156
www.bag-clasps.co.uk

Liberty
A mecca of all things beautiful and inspiring.
Great Marlborough Street
London W1B 5AH
Tel: 020 7734 1234
www.liberty.co.uk

John Lewis
Great range of haberdashery, dress-making and upholstery fabrics nationwide.
Tel: 08456 049 049
www.johnlewis.com

LIFESTYLE

Anthropologie
Inspiring lifestyle, clothing and interiors shop.
158 Regent Street
London W1B 5SW
Tel: 00800 0026 8476
www.anthropologie.eu

Labour and Wait
Simple but beautiful homeware and clothing.
85 Redchurch Street
London E2 7DJ
Tel: 020 7729 6253
www.labourandwait.co.uk

Laura Ashley
Nationwide clothing and interiors shop.
Tel: 0871 983 5999
www.lauraashley.com

Rockett St George
Quirky and individual online store selling interior goodies and gifts.
Tel: 01444 253 391
hello@rockettstgeorge.co.uk
www.rockettstgeorge.co.uk

Wickle
A mini department store full of gifts.
Tel: 01273 487 969
www.wickle.co.uk

Harlequin
Beautiful bold prints and bright colours in papers and fabrics.
www.harlequin.uk.com

WHAT ARE YOU LOOKING FOR?

Index

THANK YOU THANK YOU THANK YOU!

So many thanks must go to Lisa at Quadrille for championing this little book and for making it happen. Thanks also to Jane and Claire, and Nikki for her design skills and patience. To Gillian for reading all the words and making sure they make sense! And everyone else at Quadrille – brilliant people to work for.

To lovely Keiko for her amazing photography. This book is beautiful because of you. To Stuart and Aelia for letting me use their beautiful home – it was the perfect setting for my projects.

To all my family – Mum, Dad, Jo and family, Aunty and Uncle, Nanny and Grandad – for their support, belief, encouragement and suggestions, modelling and project testing.

Big hugs to Jake, Kirsty and Laura for listening to my ramblings, half-finished sentences and general maniacal behaviour, and to Hannah – her big ideas and passion got me where I am today.

Editorial Director Jane O'Shea
Creative Director Helen Lewis
Commissioning Editor Lisa Pendreigh
Editor Gillian Haslam
Designer Nicola Ellis, Claire Peters
Photographer Keiko Oikawa
Illustrator Christine Leech
Production Director Vincent Smith
Production Controller Aysun Hughes

Quadrille
craft

www.quadrillecraft.co.uk

First published in 2013 by
Quadrille Publishing Ltd
Alhambra House
27–31 Charing Cross Road
London WC2H 0LS
www.quadrille.co.uk

Text, project designs, artwork & illustrations
© 2013 Christine Leech
Photography © 2013 Keiko Oikawa
Design & layout © 2013 Quadrille Publishing Ltd

British Library Cataloguing-in-Publication Data
A catalogue record for this book is available from the British Library.

ISBN: 978 184949 275 1

Printed in China.